Hamlyn Kitchen Shelf

QUICK DISHES

Annette Wolter

Hamlyn
London · New York · Sydney · Toronto

This edition published by
The Hamlyn Publishing Group Limited
London · New York · Sydney · Toronto
Astronaut House, Feltham, Middlesex, England
© Copyright The Hamlyn Publishing Group Limited 1982

ISBN 0 600 32286 6

First published under the title
Die raffinierte Schnellküche
© Copyright by Gräfe und Unzer Verlag, München

First published in Great Britain
by Thomas Nelson and Sons Ltd
under the title *A Meal in a Minute*

Set in 10 on 11pt Monophoto Sabon 669
by Tameside Filmsetting Ltd,
Ashton-under-Lyne, Lancashire
Printed in Italy

Contents

Useful facts and figures

Notes on metrication

In this book quantities are given in metric and Imperial measures. Exact conversion from Imperial to metric measures does not usually give very convenient working quantities and so the metric measures have been rounded off into units of 25 grams. The table below shows the recommended equivalents.

Ounces	Approx g to nearest whole figure	Recommended conversion to nearest unit of 25
1	28	25
2	57	50
3	85	75
4	113	100
5	142	150
8	227	225
9	255	250
12	340	350
13	368	375
16 (1 lb)	454	450
18	510	500
20 ($1\frac{1}{4}$ lb)	567	575

Note: When converting quantities over 20 oz first add the appropriate figures in the centre column, then adjust to the nearest unit of 25. As a general guide, 1 kg (1000 g) equals 2.2 lb or about 2 lb 3 oz. This method of conversion gives good results in nearly all cases, although in certain pastry and cake recipes a more accurate conversion is necessary to produce a balanced recipe.

Liquid measures The millilitre has been used in this book and the following table gives a few examples.

Imperial	Approx ml to nearest whole figure	Recommended ml
$\frac{1}{4}$ pint	142	150 ml
$\frac{1}{2}$ pint	283	300 ml
$\frac{3}{4}$ pint	425	450 ml
1 pint	567	600 ml
$1\frac{1}{2}$ pints	851	900 ml
$1\frac{3}{4}$ pints	992	1000 ml (1 litre)

Spoon measures All spoon measures given in this book are level unless otherwise stated.

Can sizes At present, cans are marked with the exact (usually to the nearest whole number) metric equivalent of the Imperial weight of the contents, so we have followed this practice when giving can sizes.

Oven temperatures

The table below gives recommended equivalents.

	°C	°F	Gas Mark
Very cool	110	225	$\frac{1}{4}$
	120	250	$\frac{1}{2}$
Cool	140	275	1
	150	300	2
Moderate	160	325	3
	180	350	4
Moderately hot	190	375	5
	200	400	6
Hot	220	425	7
	230	450	8
Very hot	240	475	9

Note: When making any of the recipes in this book, only follow one set of measures as they are not interchangeable.

Basic storecupboard

The following ingredients are ideal to keep in the storecupboard for quick dishes.

bread mixes
canned fruit, corned beef
dessert topping
flour – plain and self-raising
luncheon meat
pasta, pimientos, pineapple rings/crushed
rice
sardines, soup/condensed, canned and packeted, stuffing mix, sweet and sour sauce, sweet corn kernels
tomato purée
tuna/salmon

Introduction

Everyone has at some time been faced with having to prepare a meal in minutes, whether it is for a hungry family whose appetites won't wait, or for that unexpected guest who didn't really plan to stay for supper. You will be surprised at what can be done, given a little imagination, a few basic ingredients and the help and advice of a competent, experienced and inventive cook.

Annette Wolter has put together a clever collection of recipes especially for the cook in a hurry, and though they make full use of storecupboard items, they do not compromise on flavour. In fact, as Annette Wolter hails from Germany, many of the recipes have a continental touch.

The dishes themselves range from the unashamedly simple – a Sausage goulash that takes less than 10 minutes, to the deliciously sophisticated – a Festive scampi that would do justice to a gourmet's table. There's something to suit every occasion whether it be a quick, midday snack or a full evening meal. There's no need to feel that you must have a great deal of complicated cooking equipment at your disposal. A stove or ring, a pan or two, a can opener, blender and a small refrigerator, and you are ready to start. You can choose to make a main course and follow it with fresh fruit, cheese or ice cream, or plan on whipping up a speedy pudding – a Raspberry curd cheese or Mocha mousse – while family and friends relax between courses.

The recipes in each chapter, starting with Soups right through to Desserts, are schemed into three time zones: first, dishes that can be prepared in 5–10 minutes, then those that take 10–15 minutes, and lastly, the ones that take up to 25 minutes. The preparation times are stated at the head of each recipe to make it easy to plan and time a complete menu. These times have been carefully checked; however, no two cooks work at the same speed, and you will soon find how well the timing fits into your personal 'league table'. Chilling needs to be taken into account where it occurs, as precise times for this have not been included. So much depends on individual taste and whether you have a refrigerator or a freezer. When planning a menu, it could mean making a dessert first and leaving it to chill while you organise the rest of the meal.

Quick Dishes has all the answers for those whose idea of bliss is *not* spending hours and hours in the kitchen. Get to know it well, sample some of its imaginative and appetising dishes and you will never again feel that rising tide of panic as the doorbell rings and the hands on the clock show all too clearly that there isn't time to make the meal you had planned to serve.

Note: Each recipe in this book will serve four people

Cream of asparagus soup

(Illustrated opposite)

Preparation time: 5-10 minutes

1 (298-g/10½-oz) can condensed cream of
asparagus soup
1 (312-g/11-oz) can artichoke bottoms, drained
15 g/½ oz butter
1 tablespoon single cream

Dilute and heat the asparagus soup in a covered
saucepan following the instructions on the can.
In a separate saucepan, put the artichoke bottoms
with 2 tablespoons of the soup. Add the butter,
then cover and simmer over a low heat. When the
soup is thoroughly heated through, stir in the
cream. Pour into cups or individual bowls and
add the cooked artichokes in the butter just before
serving.

Pea soup with sausage

(Illustrated opposite)

Preparation time: 5-10 minutes

1 (298-g/10½-oz) can cream of pea soup
1 small onion
a little butter or oil
1 tablespoon single cream
2–4 smoked chipolata or Frankfurter sausages,
cut into chunks
2 tablespoons chopped chives

Heat the pea soup in a covered saucepan following the instructions on the can. Meanwhile, peel
and chop the onion finely and fry in a little butter
or oil until crisp. Add the cream, fried onion and
sausage to the soup and allow to heat through.
Garnish each portion with chives before serving.

Cream of onion soup

(Illustrated opposite)

Preparation time: 5-10 minutes

1 (298-g/10½-oz) can condensed cream of
onion soup
15 g/½ oz butter
1 onion, peeled and cut into rings
1 green pepper, deseeded and cut into rings
1 (200-g/7-oz) can corned beef

Dilute and heat the onion soup in a covered
saucepan following the instructions on the can.
Melt the butter in a frying pan and gently fry the
onion and pepper rings. Dice the corned beef and
heat through in the soup. Pour into 4 individual
bowls and garnish each with onion and pepper
rings.

Variations

Bacon and corn soup Lightly fry 75 g/3 oz
chopped bacon and add to the hot soup with
50–100 g/2–4 oz well-drained canned corn kernels.

Pea and ham soup Heat 225 g/8 oz frozen peas in
the soup and add 100 g/4 oz chopped cooked
ham. Heat through thoroughly before serving.
Well-drained canned baby carrots or chopped
Continental sausage are also good alternatives to
add to the soup, or simply stir in 4 tablespoons
single cream just before serving.

Clockwise from top: Pea soup with sausage; Cream of
asparagus soup (recipes above left); Cream of tomato
soup; Chicken soup with curried cream (page 10);
Cream of onion soup (recipe above).

Chicken soup with curried cream

(Illustrated on page 9)

Preparation time: 5-10 minutes

1 (298-g/10½-oz) can condensed cream of
chicken soup
300 g/11 oz frozen peas
100 ml/4 fl oz double cream
1–2 teaspoons curry paste (according to taste)

Dilute and heat the chicken soup in a covered
saucepan following the instructions on the can.
Add the frozen peas, replace the lid and continue
to heat through for a further 5 minutes. Meanwhile, whip the cream until stiff, and gently fold
in the curry paste. Serve the soup in 4 individual
cups or bowls and garnish each serving with a
tablespoon of the curried cream.

Variations

*The following can be used to enrich any
ready-prepared cream soup:*

Add a little cream to the soup with 4 tablespoons
frozen chopped parsley just before serving.

Add 225 g/8 oz diced, cooked chicken or veal
with a few strips of canned pimiento to the soup
and heat through.

Add 1 (241-g/8½-oz) can asparagus tips, drained,
100 g/4 oz canned tomatoes, drained and sliced,
and 4 tablespoons white wine to the soup and
gently heat through.

Add 100 g/4 oz chopped smoked ham or cooked
chicken and 225 g/8 oz frozen peas to the soup
and heat through for a further 5 minutes before
serving.

Cream of tomato soup

(Illustrated on page 9)

Preparation time: 5-10 minutes

1 (298-g/10½-oz) can condensed cream of
tomato soup
15 g/½ oz butter
50 g/2 oz white bread, cut into small cubes
generous pinch of garlic salt
1 tablespoon chopped parsley

Dilute and heat the tomato soup in a saucepan
following the instructions on the can. Meanwhile,
melt the butter in a frying pan and fry the bread
cubes, turning occasionally until golden brown.
Sprinkle these croûtons with the garlic salt and
transfer them from the frying pan to drain on
absorbent kitchen paper. Just before serving,
sprinkle each bowl of soup with parsley and top
with the garlic croûtons.

Variations

Shrimp or crabmeat soup Add 150 g/5 oz canned
shrimp or crabmeat, drained, to the soup before
heating. Continue as above.

Cold cucumber soup

Preparation time: 5-10 minutes

1 medium cucumber
1 (184-g/6½-oz) can pimientos, drained
¼ teaspoon salt
pinch each of celery and garlic salt
dash of Worcestershire sauce
1 tablespoon paprika pepper
3 (142-ml/5-fl oz) cartons natural yogurt
4 tablespoons chopped parsley

Peel and chop the cucumber into chunks. Place in
a blender with the remaining ingredients except
the parsley and liquidise until blended. Stir in the
parsley.

Bean soup

Preparation time: 5-10 minutes

---

1 (425-g/15-oz) can haricot beans
250 g/9 oz canned peeled tomatoes, drained
600 ml/1 pint canned tomato juice
300 ml/½ pint dry white wine
½ teaspoon salt
1 teaspoon chilli powder, or to taste

Drain the beans; chop the tomatoes. Mix the tomato juice with the white wine in a saucepan and add the beans and chopped tomato. Season with salt and chilli powder, cover and heat through thoroughly but gently.

Lobster soup

Preparation time: 10-15 minutes

---

1 (435-g/15¼-oz) can lobster bisque
1 (225-g/8-oz) can crabmeat
1 egg, hard-boiled
4 tablespoons single cream
1 tablespoon brandy

Prepare the lobster bisque following the instructions on the can. Drain the crabmeat and rinse quickly under running cold water. Flake the meat

into the soup and heat through. Peel and finely chop the egg. Mix together the cream and brandy. Take the soup off the heat and stir in the cream mixture. Serve garnished with chopped egg.

Onion soup

Preparation time: 10-15 minutes

---

1 (298-g/10½-oz) can condensed onion soup
100 ml/4 fl oz white wine
8 thin slices French bread
50 g/2 oz butter
garlic salt
25 g/1 oz cheese, grated

Set the oven at hot (230 C, 450 F, Gas Mark 8) or heat the grill to maximum. Dilute and heat the onion soup following the instructions on the can. Stir in the wine. Spread the bread slices with half the butter, sprinkle each one with a little garlic salt and toast lightly. Pour the soup into 4 individual ovenproof bowls, place 2 pieces of toast on each serving and sprinkle with cheese. Dot with the remaining butter and bake for 8 minutes or until the top is browned and bubbling.

Onion soup.

Curry cream soup

(Illustrated opposite)

Preparation time: 10-15 minutes

1 tablespoon oil
2 level teaspoons plain flour
900 ml/1½ pints beef or chicken stock,
made from stock cubes if necessary
salt and pepper
450 g/1 lb apple purée
15 g/½ oz butter
2 level teaspoons curry powder, or to taste
75 ml/3 fl oz single cream
1 (184-g/6½-oz) can pimientos,
drained and chopped

Heat the oil in a large saucepan and add the flour. Stir with a wooden spoon, then add the stock slowly, stirring all the time. Season, if necessary. Bring to the boil, stirring constantly until the soup thickens. Lower the heat, stir in the apple purée and allow it to warm through.

Meanwhile, melt the butter in a small pan, add the curry powder and mix well. Add this to the soup with the cream. Remove from the heat, pour into individual bowls and scatter each with pimiento before serving.

Spinach soup

Preparation time: 10-15 minutes

900 ml/1½ pints milk
salt and pepper
300–450 g/11 oz–1 lb frozen chopped spinach
2 egg yolks
100 ml/4 fl oz single cream
pinch garlic salt
4 tablespoons grated cheese

Put the milk in a saucepan, season with salt and pepper and bring slowly to the boil. Add the frozen spinach, stir, then cover the saucepan and cook gently for 8 minutes. Stir the egg yolks into the cream and add the garlic salt. Remove the pan

Curry cream soup (recipe above); Corned beef snack (page 50).

from the heat and add the egg mixture to the soup. Return the pan to the heat and stir until the soup thickens, but do not allow it to boil. Serve sprinkled with the grated cheese.

Speedy goulash soup

Preparation time: 15-25 minutes

25 g/1 oz butter
1 small onion, finely chopped
350 g/12 oz minced beef
pepper and paprika pepper to taste
1 rounded tablespoon plain flour
600 ml/1 pint beef stock, made from stock
cubes if necessary
300 ml/½ pint canned tomato juice
250 ml/8 fl oz single cream
2 tablespoons chopped parsley

Melt the butter in a large saucepan and fry the onion until transparent. Add the meat and lightly fry, stirring with a fork all the time so it browns evenly. Sprinkle generously with pepper and paprika and then the flour and continue to stir until well mixed and the meat is cooked. Slowly add the stock and bring to the boil, stirring all the time. Allow to boil for a couple of minutes. Add the tomato juice and cream and heat through gently. Sprinkle with parsley before serving.

Vegetable noodle soup

Preparation time: 15-25 minutes

900 ml/1½ pints beef or chicken stock,
made from stock cubes if necessary
50 g/2 oz small noodles or pasta shapes
1 (450-g/1-lb) packet frozen chopped mixed
vegetables
salt and pepper
4 tablespoons grated Parmesan cheese

In a saucepan, bring the stock to the boil. Add the pasta and the vegetables and allow them to cook through over a low heat. Season, if necessary, and sprinkle with grated cheese before serving.

Fish and shellfish

Shrimp vols-au-vent

(Illustrated below)

Preparation time: 10-15 minutes

---

50 g/2 oz Edam cheese
4 individual vol-au-vent cases
1 (198-g/7-oz) can shrimps
200 g/7 oz canned mussels
100 g/4 oz canned carrots, diced
juice of ½ lemon
a little caviare or lumpfish roe to garnish
(optional)

Set the oven at hot (230 C, 450 F, Gas Mark 8) or heat the grill to maximum. Slice half the cheese into four and put one piece of cheese in the bottom of each pastry case. Place in the oven just to heat through. Drain and rinse the shrimps under cold running water, reserving 8 to garnish. Drain the mussels and carrots. Cut the rest of the cheese into strips. Mix together the shrimps, mussels and carrots and fill the warm pastry cases with this mixture. Top with the cheese strips and place in the oven or under grill for 2–3 minutes. Garnish each with two of the reserved shrimps and sprinkle with caviare or lumpfish roe, if liked, before serving.

Festive scampi

(Illustrated opposite)

Preparation time: 10-15 minutes

---

15 g/½ oz butter
4 eggs
pinch each salt and pepper
4 large slices white bread
4 slices smoked salmon
4 scampi, cooked and peeled
1 tablespoon caviare or lumpfish roe (optional)

Melt the butter in a pan over gentle heat. Meanwhile, whisk the eggs in a bowl, season, then lightly scramble in the hot butter. When just set, divide the egg mixture between the bread slices. Roll up each slice of smoked salmon and place one on each slice of bread. Add one scampi to each and garnish, if liked, with a little caviare or lumpfish roe. Serve with Pea soup with sausage (see page 8) and follow with Cherry nut mousse (see page 66).

Below: Shrimp vols-au-vent; *Opposite*: Festive scampi.

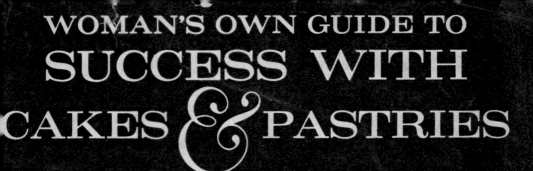

WOMAN'S OWN GUIDE TO
SUCCESS WITH
CAKES & PASTRIES

16-PAGE FREE SUPPLEMENT EDITED BY JANE BEATON

PRESENTED WITH WOMAN'S OWN, OCTOBER 3RD, 1964

The warm, spicy scents of home baking, and the family's smiles of anticipation make the work of preparation a pleasure. So here are some tested recipes and methods for favourite cakes and pastries, for party fare, lunch boxes and for special celebrations. Plus plenty of variations to give you a large range of types and flavours and step-by-step instructions to make certain of success

success with your CAKES

RUBBING IN

For the basic mixture you require: 8 oz. self raising flour, $\frac{1}{2}$ level teasp. salt, 4 oz. margarine, 4 oz. sugar, 2 standard eggs, 2 tbsp. milk.

Sift dry ingredients into large bowl. Add margarine and rub in until mixture is like breadcrumbs. Add sugar, fruit if desired, and any other flavourings. Mix to fairly stiff dropping consistency with eggs and milk. *Secret of success:* careful rubbing in of fat into flour.

Large cakes: Bake in centre of mod. oven. Mark 4, 350 deg. 1-1¼ hrs. or until firm.

Small cakes: Bake in upper part mod. oven, Mark 6, 400 deg. for 15-20 mins.

Variations: Family Fruit Cake (see top right). Add $\frac{1}{2}$ level teasp. mixed spice to dry ingredients. Stir in 4 oz. sultanas and 4 oz. currants, cleaned and dried, and 1 oz. chopped, mixed peel. Turn into prepared 2 lb. loaf tin and bake.

CHOCOLATE CHIP

Add 1 teasp. vanilla essence and 1 pkt. chocolate dots to bowl before mixing with eggs and milk. Turn into prepared 6-in. round cake tin. Bake as for large cake.

PINEAPPLE CAKE

Add 3 oz. roughly chopped, glacé pineapple to rubbed-in mixture. Turn into prepared 6-in. round cake tin and place 1 oz. glacé pineapple cut into large segments over top. Bake as above.

FRUIT AND NUT SQUARE

Add 1 teasp. almond essence, 4 oz. seedless raisins, cleaned and dried, and 2 oz. roughly chopped, blanched almonds, to bowl, before mixing with eggs and milk. Turn into prepared 6-in. square cake tin and bake.

ORANGE SPICE CAKE

Add 1 teasp. mixed spice and the coarsely grated rind of an orange to the basic mixture. Turn into prepared 6-in. tin and bake as above. When cold coat with orange glacé icing.

ROCK BUNS

Add an extra 2 oz. flour when sifting into bowl. Add granulated sugar instead of castor, also 4 oz. ready-cleaned, mixed dried fruit. Put mixture in patty tins or in rounds on baking sheets. Bake as for small cakes. Makes 18-20.

CHERRY BUNS

Halve 4 oz. glacé-cherries, and add to rubbed-in mixture together with 1 teasp. vanilla essence. Bake as for small cakes. Makes 18-20.

COCONUT

Add 2 oz. dessicated coconut to rubbed-in mixture. Put into prepared patty tins and bake. Makes 18.

ALMOND SPICE

Add 1 level teasp. powdered mixed spice to dry ingredients when sifting. Add 1 oz. ground almonds and 1 teasp. almond essence before mixing with egg and milk. Turn into prepared patty tins and bake. Makes 18.

MARMALADE MOUNDIES

Add 2 tbsp. marmalade and only 2 oz. sugar to rubbed-in mixture. Put into prepared patty tins and bake. Makes 18.

Here's a delicious Family Fruit Cake. Easy to make when you follow my step-by-step instructions

TEA-TIME SCONES

Shown on our cover. Add 8 oz. self-raising flour to dry ingredients when sifting. Mix to soft dough with about ¼ pt. milk. Turn mixture on to floured board and roll out to ½-in. in thickness. Cut into 24 rounds, using plain 2-in. cutter. Brush with beaten egg or milk. Put on to 2 greased baking sheets and bake near top of mod. oven. Mark 7, 425 deg. for 10-15 mins. Split, butter and spread with jam.

FRUIT SHORTCAKE

Make as for tea-time scones but divide dough into two pieces. Roll each piece into 8-in. round and place on two separate baking sheets. Dot each with 1 oz. butter. Bake as for scones, then turn on to a wire rack to cool. Sandwich together with whipped cream and any fruit. Top with more.

RAISIN CAKE

Add 8 oz. cleaned, stoned raisins to the basic mixture. Turn into a prepared 6-in. cake tin. Brush the top with water and sprinkle with castor sugar. Bake as above.

FAMILY FRUIT CAKE

1. Grease and line base of 2-lb. loaf tin. Sift flour, salt and spice, rub in fat. Stir in the sugar

2. Add the prepared sultanas, currants and chopped peel. Mix ingredients well together

3. Make a well in centre. Break the eggs, one at a time, into a basin and add to the mixture. Stir briskly with wooden spoon

4. Add sufficient milk to give a slightly stiff consistency

5. Put into the prepared tin and hollow out centre. Bake

CREAMING

Here are the best recipes for your favourite rich cakes. Luscious layer cakes, fruity cakes for special occasions and an unusual Apple Cake; as well as quick-to-make-and-bake buns and cup cakes. They all keep well—if your family gives you half a chance to store them—in tins

Creamed cakes are those that have a high proportion of fat to flour and, therefore, need to have the fat and sugar creamed together first. For easy mixing, make sure the fat is just soft, before you start. If kept in a cold place, put out in the kitchen about half an hour before making your cake.

BASIC CREAMING RECIPE

You require: 4 oz. self-raising flour, pinch salt, 4 oz. butter or magarine, 4 oz. castor sugar, 2 standard eggs.

Sift flour and salt. Cream fat and sugar together until light. Add eggs. Fold in flour.

Secrets of success: Maximum creaming, eggs well beaten in, careful folding in of flour. *Baking.* **Sandwich cakes:** Bake in centre moderate oven, Mark 4, 350 deg. for 25-30 mins. **Large rich cakes:** Bake in centre of slow to moderate oven, Mark 3, 335 deg. for 1-1¼ hrs. **Large, not-so-rich cakes:** Bake in centre of moderate oven, Mark 4, 350 deg., for 1 hr.

Small cakes: Bake in upper part of moderate oven, Mark 5, 375 deg. for 20-25 mins.

VICTORIA SANDWICH

(See right.) Make as for basic method, adding 1 tbsp. warm water and a few drops of vanilla essence after flour is added. Sandwich together with 2 tbsp. raspberry jam. Sprinkle top with castor sugar.

CHERRY CAKE

Make double basic recipe. Add an extra 4 oz. of self-raising flour. Beat 1 teasp. vanilla essence into creamed mixture. Stir 6 oz. cherries into flour before adding to mixture. Turn into a 7-in. round cake tin. Bake as large, rich cakes.

ORANGE AND CHOCOLATE LAYER

(Shown on our cover.) Make twice basic recipe. Remove one third mixture, and stir into it 1 level tbsp. cocoa blended with 1 tbsp. hot water. Fold grated rind 1 orange into plain mixture. Divide the orange mixture between two 6-in. tins and bake. Bake chocolate layer in one 6-in. tin. Sandwich with butter cream. Decorate as shown.

RICH FRUIT CAKE

Make double quantity of basic recipe. Before mixing in flour, add to it 3 oz. fine semolina, 12 oz. cleaned currants, 12 oz. cleaned sultanas, 4 oz. chopped mixed peel, 4 oz. glacé cherries, halved, 2 oz. ground almonds and the grated rind of half a lemon. Put mixture into an 8-in. square cake tin which has been lined with double layers of greaseproof

Tea-time treat, Pound Cake with sliced almond topping

4

Feather-light Victoria Sandwich, dusted with sugar

CREAMED MIXTURES

1. Grease and line the bases of two 7-in. sandwich tins. Sift flour and salt. Cream butter and sugar until fluffy

2. Break eggs, one at a time, into basin and add to creamed butter and sugar, beating well after adding each egg

paper. Bake in centre of slow oven. Mark 2, 310 deg. for 2 hrs. Reduce heat to Mark 1, 290 deg. for further hour.

Cool, then wrap in grease-proof paper and store in an air-tight tin for at least a week before icing.

APPLE CAKE

Make basic recipe but use an extra 4 oz. self-raising flour. Sift level teasp. of powered cinnamon into flour and add 1 peeled and grated cooking apple (about $\frac{1}{2}$ lb.) into the flour. Turn the mixture into prepared 6-in. round cake tin and bake as for not-so-rich large cakes.

COFFEE RING

Make the basic recipe, but add an extra 2 oz. self-raising flour. Dissolve 1 rounded teasp. instant coffee in 1 tbsp. boiling water, and beat into creamed butter or margarine and sugar. Turn the mixture into greased 7-in. ring tin and bake as for large, rich cakes.

POUND CAKE

(See picture left.) Make basic recipe. Stir 4 oz. cleaned,

dried, mixed fruit into the flour before you begin mixing. Blanch $\frac{1}{2}$ oz. almonds and cut them into fine slices. Turn mixture into prepared 1 lb. loaf tin, make the top smooth and then sprinkle with the prepared almonds. Bake as for large, rich cakes.

FAIRY CAKES

Stir 2 oz. currants into flour and add 1 teasp. vanilla essence to basic mixture. Put mixture into 12 small paper cake cases and bake as for small cakes.

LITTLE STRUESAL BUNS

Make basic mixture and put into 12 small paper cake cases. Mix 1$\frac{1}{2}$ oz. brown sugar and 1$\frac{1}{2}$ level teasp. powdered cinnamon together. Sprinkle over the tops of the cakes and bake as for small cakes.

CUP CAKES

Make basic mixture and flavour according to choice. Bake in 12 small paper cake cases. Cool and top with glacé icing.

3. Add sifted flour, $\frac{1}{3}$ at a time, and fold in lightly, using wooden or metal spoon

4. Finally, stir in warm water and vanilla essence. The mixture should be of a dropping consistency

5. Divide mixture equally between two tins and spread evenly. Bake

MELTING AND WHISKING

These are the two methods used by skilled cooks to achieve those light-as-air, almost untouched by hand cakes. Use the melting method for ginger-bread, date and walnut cake, or delicious, sweet honey and nut. Use the whisking method for light Swiss rolls, and sponges. If you follow my basic recipes you can't go wrong

BASIC MELTING RECIPE

You require: 8 oz. plain flour, ½ level teasp. salt, 2 level teasp. ground ginger, 1 lever teasp. bicarb. of soda, 4 oz. butter, 4 oz. soft brown sugar, 4 oz. golden syrup, 2 standard eggs, a little milk to mix.

Sift dry ingredients into a large bowl. Put butter, sugar and syrup into pan. Heat until butter is melted, then add to dry ingredients together with beaten eggs. Beat well. Add a little warm milk, if necessary, to give fairly stiff, pouring consistency. Pour mixture into 7-in. round cake tin, bake in centre mod. to slow oven, Mark 3, 335 deg. for 1¼-1½ hrs. *Secret of success:* Mix quickly; put in oven immediately.

PARKIN

Add 4 oz. fine oatmeal to dry ingredients, and 1 tbsp. black treacle to melting mixture. Mix to a pouring consistency with more warm milk.

Bake in 8-in. square cake tin and store in a tin for a week before using. Spread with butter when serving.

DATE AND WALNUT

Add 4 oz. chopped dates and 2 oz. chopped walnuts to flour before mixing. Bake in 7-in. round tin as above.

HONEY AND NUT

Add 2 oz. chopped blanched almonds to flour and 2 tbsp. clear honey to melting mixture. Make and bake as for basic method.

UPSIDE DOWN CAKE

(Below.) Melt 1 oz. butter and 2 oz. brown sugar. Pour in base of 7-in. square cake tin. Arrange pieces of fruit, e.g., pineapple and cherries in base. Cover with basic mixture. Bake 45-50 mins.

LEMON SPICE BREAD

Add 1 teasp. mixed spice to flour with grated rind 1

lemon. Put in 1-lb. loaf tin, bake as for basic method.

BASIC WHISKING RECIPE

You require: 3 standard eggs, 3 oz. castor sugar, pinch salt, 3 oz. self-raising flour, 1 tbsp. warm water.

Whisk eggs and sugar until thick and creamy, and until mixture will retain the impression of whisk for 5 seconds. Carefully fold in sifted flour with metal spoon, then fold in warm water. *Secret of success:* Very thorough whisking, really careful folding.

SWISS ROLL

Put mixture into prepared Swiss roll tin, 7½ ins. x 11½ ins. Bake in upper part of mod. oven, Mark 7, 425 deg. for about 7 mins, or until golden. Turn on to sugared paper, trim edges. Spread with 2 tbsp. warm jam, and roll up using paper to help. Leave rolled until cool.

JAM AND CREAM SPONGE

Put basic mixture into 6-in. round cake tin, bake in centre of mod. oven, Mark 3, 335 deg. for 45-60 mins., or until firm. Leave to cool in tin for 2 mins. Turn on to sugared paper.

When cool, split and spread with raspberry jam and whipped fresh cream. Sandwich together.

ORANGE FLUFF

Make basic recipe and bake as for Jam and Cream Sponge. Split cake in half, and sandwich together with orange flavoured butter cream. Spread sides with more butter cream, coat in finely crushed biscuit crumbs.

Fruity Upside Down Cake for lunch or tea

For celebrations—fruit cake to cut and small iced sponges

Here's a short guide to easy cake decorating. Follow my suggestions for some new ways of topping your favourite cakes

DECORATING

Cakes can be iced and decorated with a variety of icings and toppings. Rich fruit cakes should first be brushed top and sides with hot apricot glaze, then covered with Almond Paste. Plain and sponge cakes can be iced with Glacé Icing, Butter Cream, or the toppings given below or overleaf.

ROYAL ICING

You require: 5 egg whites, juice 1 lemon, $2\frac{1}{2}$ lbs. sifted icing sugar, 6 drops glycerine.

Put egg whites into a large bowl, and beat lightly. Add sifted icing sugar, 2 tbsp. at a time, beating well.

As mixture stiffens, add a little lemon juice. Finally beat in glycerine. Icing should coat back of spoon.

ALMOND PASTE

You require: 1 lb. castor sugar, 1 lb. icing sugar, sifted, 1 lb. ground almonds, 2 large eggs, juice 1 lemon, almond essence.

Put castor sugar, icing sugar and ground almonds into a large bowl. Beat the eggs in another bowl and add to almonds. Add lemon juice and few drops almond essence to taste. Knead mixture with the hands until it forms a ball.

GLACE ICING

You require: 4 oz. sifted icing sugar, 1 tbsp. warm water, flavouring, colouring.

Put icing sugar into basin, place over a pan of hot water. Gradually add the warm water and beat well with wooden spoon. Beat in flavouring and colouring. Icing should coat the back of a wooden spoon.

VARIATIONS

Coffee: Blend 1 level teasp. instant coffee with warm water before mixing.

Lemon or Orange: Substitute lemon or orange juice for the warm water and add a yellow or orange colouring.

Chocolate: Blend 1 rounded teasp. cocoa powder with 1 dessertsp. hot water.

American Frosting: Put 8 oz. gran. sugar and 4 tbsp. water into pan. Dissolve slowly over very low heat. Make sure no sugar crystals remain. Boil mixture to 240 deg. or until a little dropped into a bowl of cold water forms a ball. Remove from the heat, and allow the bubbles to subside. Meanwhile, whisk an egg white until it looks dry. Continue whisking, at same time, pour syrup in a steady stream on to the egg white. Continue beat-

ing until mixture begins to thicken. Pour over cake.

Butter Icing: Beat together 4 oz. unsalted butter and 8 oz. sifted icing sugar. Flavour.

Fudge Icing: Melt 1 oz. unsalted butter, $1\frac{1}{2}$ oz. plain chocolate and 1 tbsp. evaporated milk or cream in basin over pan of hot water. Cook. Beat in 1 teasp. vanilla essence and sifted icing sugar to make spreading mixture.

APRICOT GLAZE

Heat 2 tbsp. apricot jam and 1 tbsp. water. Sieve, then return to pan. Bring to boil. Use.

CHRISTENING CAKE

See picture above.

Brush top and sides of Rich Fruit Cake with boiling Apricot Glaze. Cover with Almond Paste. Leave to dry. Cover cake with $\frac{3}{4}$ Royal Icing. Leave to dry for 1-2 days. Keep remaining icing in a screwtop jar until required. Place iced cake on board.

Fit icing bag with star nozzle, pipe rosettes as in picture. Tie ribbon round edge and place flowers in centre.

Serve Little Iced Cakes for the children. Coat sponge cakes with glacé icing and decorate with butter cream.

More toppings overleaf.

TOPPINGS are the glamour

touches that win you admiring compliments from your family and friends. Here are some of my favourite ways to decorate cakes—they're all effective and wonderfully simple to do. So if you've got a few spare minutes after your next baking session why not try out one of these ideas and give your family a treat?

RASPBERRY MARSHMALLOW HATS

Melt 1 tbsp. raspberry jam and 1 oz. marshmallows in a basin over a pan of hot water. Cool. Beat together 2 oz. butter and 5 oz. icing sugar. Beat in the melted marsh-mallows and jam. Cool and

spread or pipe on to cakes. Decorate centre with whole marshmallow.

ORANGE FLUFFS

Coat top of Orange Fluff (page 6) with orange glacé icing. Allow to dry for a few minutes, then pipe more glacé icing in a pattern over top.

TUTTI FRUTTI TOPPING

Heat $\frac{1}{2}$ lb. sugar, 4 tbsps. of water and 2 tbsp. of clear honey together until sugar is dissolved. Boil to 240 deg. F. or until a little dropped into cold water forms a ball. Cover Honey Cake (page 6) with 2 oz. of glacé cherries, 2 ozs. of

8

whole blanched almonds, 2 oz. seedless raisins, and $\frac{1}{2}$ oz. chopped angelica. Allow bubbles of boiling mixture to settle, then pour slowly over the fruit.

FROSTED COFFEE RING

Coat Coffee Ring Cake (page 5) with American Frosting.

Allow to coat smoothly. Decorate with halved walnuts. Fill centres with small rounds of almond paste, which have previously been decorated with halved walnuts.

PEANUT AND LEMON

Beat together 2 tbsp. of peanut butter and 2 oz. un-

salted butter. Add 6 oz. of sifted icing sugar and lemon juice to taste. Make the basic sandwich mixture (see page 4) and flavour with lemon rind. Bake in lined Swiss roll tin 11 in. by 4 in. Cut in half. Sandwich together with half mixture, spread rest on top. Decorate with halved peanuts and crystallized lemon slices.

success with PASTRIES

Melt in the mouth shortcrust, and crisp, layered rough puff pastry are the bases of these delicious recipes. Here is a wide selection of desserts, individual cakes and tartlets, filled with fruits and jams

SHORTCRUST PASTRY

1. Sift flour and salt. Cut fat into flour in walnut-sized pieces for easier rubbing in

2. Using tips of fingers, rub fat into flour until mixture resembles fairly fine breadcrumbs

3. Make a well in the centre and add cold water. Using a round bladed knife mix to a firm dough

4. Knead lightly to remove cracks and roll out on lightly floured board, using short, brisk strokes

SHORTCRUST

The most popular and quick-to-make of the pastries. It can be used for pies, flans and tartlets, and flavours such as mixed spice and grated lemon or orange rind can be added for variety.

If the weather is very hot, and the fat rather soft, use $\frac{1}{2}$ oz. less, otherwise the pastry will become sticky and difficult to handle. The dry rubbed-in mixture can be stored in a cool place in a screw-top jar and used as required. Save time by making a double quantity and store half to use later.

Basic recipe You require:— 8 oz. plain flour; 1 level teasp. salt; 4 oz. butter OR 2 oz. margarine and 2 oz. lard or white vegetable fat; 4 tbsp. cold water.

Sift the flour and salt into a bowl. Rub in the butter or mixture of fats until mix resembles breadcrumbs. Add water and lightly form mixture into a dough with finger tips.

Secrets of success: Keep everything cool. Mix with a knife. Use the right amount of water. Roll out lightly.

PLUM PIE

Fill an 8 in. round pie plate with $1\frac{1}{2}$ lb. of washed plums. Sprinkle 4 oz. of granulated sugar over when half the plums are added. Roll pastry into round about 10 ins. across. Trim edges of pastry and use to line edge of dish. Damp the edges. Place pastry round over top of plums and seal the edges. Knock up with the back of a knife and flute edges. Bake in the upper part of moderately hot oven, Mark 6, 400 deg. for 35-40 mins. or until pastry is golden and plums tender.

ALMOND MAIDS

Line two 9-hole patty tins with rounds of shortcrust pastry. Prick bases well. Cream together 4 oz. of butter and 4 oz. of castor sugar until light and fluffy. Beat in 2 eggs, one at a time, beating well after each addition. Fold in 2 oz. sifted self-raising flour, 4 oz. of ground almonds and 1 teasp. of almond essence. Put half a teasp. of raspberry jam into each lined tin, and cover with a heaped teasp. of almond mixture. Make the top smooth. Place 5 halved blanched almonds over the top of each and bake in the upper part of a moderate oven, Mark 5, 375 deg. for 25-30 mins.

FRUIT SLICES

Make double quantity of basic recipe. Use half to line a Swiss Roll tin $7\frac{1}{2}$ by $11\frac{1}{2}$ ins. Prick base well. Spread base with 4 oz. sultanas, 2 oz. currants, and 2 oz. of seedless raisins, all washed. Sprinkle with 3 oz. of soft brown sugar and the finely grated rind and juice of 1 lemon.

Bake in the upper part of a moderately hot oven, Mark 7, 425 deg. for 25-30 mins. When cold cut into slices about 2 ins. wide.

BANANA APRICOT TART

Make double the quantity of shortcrust pastry. Use half to line an 8 in. round pie plate. Prick base well. Spread with 4 tbsp. of apricot jam. Slice 4 bananas over the top and sprinkle with the juice of half a lemon and some grated rind. Cover the bananas with the remaining pastry, and seal edges well. Bake in the upper

Almond Maids with a plum-filled pie

ROUGH PUFF

This is one of the richer pastries, and is best made with a firm butter or margarine. It requires light handling and careful, even rolling. Use very cold water, preferably iced, for mixing. The rich golden colour of the pastry and the crisp even layers make a tempting picture when used to make dinner or tea-time sweets.

Basic recipe You require:— 8 oz. plain flour, 1 level teasp. salt, 6 oz. firm butter or margarine, cold water to mix.

Sift flour into large bowl, together with salt. Cut fat in large pieces, add to the flour and mix lightly. Mix to a fairly soft dough with cold water, without breaking lumps of fat.

Roll dough into long strip about $\frac{1}{4}$-in. in thickness, keeping the edges straight. Turn $\frac{1}{3}$ pastry up from base, and another $\frac{1}{3}$ down from the top. Press edges well to seal. Give the pastry a half turn, clockwise, repeat rolling and folding processes three times more. Allow pastry to rest in a cool place or refrigerator for 15 mins. between each rolling. *Secret of success:* Allow the required resting time between rollings. Put finished pastry into cool place for at least $\frac{1}{2}$ hr. before using as required.

part of a moderate oven, Mark 6, 400 deg. for 25-30 mins. or until golden brown.

TREACLE TART

Line a 9 in. plate with basic pastry. Prick base well. Decorate edge. Spoon 4 good tbsp. of golden syrup over the pastry and spread over the base of the plate. Sprinkle with 1 oz. of crushed cornflakes. Bake in the upper part of a moderately hot oven, Mark 6, 400 deg. until pastry is golden. Serve hot or cold.

FLAN PASTRY

You require: 8 oz. plain flour; pinch of salt; 5 oz. butter; 1 oz. castor sugar; 1 egg yolk; 2-3 tbsp. cold water to mix.

Sift the flour and salt into a large bowl. Rub in the butter until the mixture looks like breadcrumbs. Add the castor sugar and mix to a fairly stiff dough with the egg yolk and water. Use as required.

PEACH FLAN

Use 1 quantity of pastry to line an 8 in. flan case which has been placed on a baking sheet. Prick base well. Place a sheet of oiled greaseproof paper over the pastry and fill centre with baking beans. Bake in the upper part of a moderately hot oven, Mark 6, 400 deg. for about 25 mins. Remove the paper and beans after 20 mins.

Drain a 16 oz. can of peaches, reserving the juice. Arrange the peaches over the base of the flan case. Make the juice up to $\frac{1}{4}$ pint with water. Add the juice of half a lemon. Blend 1 teasp. of arrowroot with a little of the juice. Put remaining juice into a small saucepan and bring to the boil. Pour on to blended arrowroot. Return to pan. Bring to boil, stirring, cook for 2 mins. Pour over the peaches.

CUSTARD TART

Make half the basic recipe, and use to line a 6 in. sandwich tin. Prick the base well. Put a piece of oiled greaseproof paper in the centre and fill with baking beans. Bake in the upper part of a moderately hot oven, Mark 6, 400 deg., for 15 mins. Remove the paper and beans and cook further 5 mins. Heat $\frac{1}{2}$ pint of milk to blood heat. Beat 2 standard eggs in a basin, together with 1 oz. of castor sugar. Pour the warm milk on to the beaten eggs and mix well. Strain the mixture into the flan case, sprinkle a little grated nutmeg over the top. Reduce oven to slow-moderate, Mark 3, 335 deg., and put tart into centre of oven for 35-40 mins. or until the custard is set.

VOL AU VENT

Roll pastry out into a 6-in. round, $\frac{1}{2}$ in. thick. Cut a 4 in. round in the centre, but cutting only half way through pastry. Place pastry on wetted baking sheet. Mark the centre round or lid in diamond shapes with the blade of a wet, pointed knife. Put pastry into a cold place, a refrigerator if possible, for 30 mins. before baking.

Brush the top with beaten egg yolk, and bake in upper part of hot oven, Mark 8, 450 deg. for 25-30 mins., or until well risen and golden brown.

1. Sift flour and salt. Cut fat into ¾ inch cubes into a bowl

2. Stir fat into flour. Mix with cold water to soft, not sticky, dough

3. On fairly well-floured board, roll out to rectangle 8×15 in. Carefully fold the top ⅓ down to centre

4. Carefully fold bottom ⅓ up over the centre

5. Seal open ends. Give ½ turn before repeating rolling and folding 3 times, giving 4 rollings in all. Use as required

ROUGH PUFF PASTRY continued

Remove from oven and remove 'lid' of pastry. Remove and discard any soft pastry from inside vol au vent. Fill centre with whipped cream and decorate with canned, sliced peaches and cherries or fruit of choice. Replace 'lid' and serve.

ECCLES CAKES

Make basic quantity of rough puff pastry. Roll out to ¼ in. in thickness. Cut into 4-in. rounds with plain cutter. Cream together 1 oz. butter, 1 oz. soft brown sugar. Add 2 oz. cleaned currants, ½ oz. chopped, mixed peel and ½ level teasp. mixed spice. Mix well, then put same amount in centre of each pastry round.

Dampen edges and gather them together, pressing well. Turn the cakes over and place on greased baking sheet. Make 2 snips in top of each with scissors, and brush over with milk. Sprinkle with a little sugar. Bake in upper part mod. hot oven, Mark 7, 425 deg. for about 20 mins.

JAM PUFFS

Roll 1 quantity of pastry out to ¼-in. thick, cut into 4-in. squares. Place teasp. of firm jam in centre of each. Dampen edges and turn one corner over the jam to meet the opposite corner, forming a triangle.

Press edges together and flake with back of knife.

Put on to greased baking sheet and brush with water. Sprinkle with granulated sugar. Bake in upper part of hot oven, Mark 7, 425 deg., about 20 mins.

LITTLE FRUIT PIES

Roll 1 quantity of pastry out to just under ¼-in. thick. Cut out 12 rounds to fit tartlet tins. Prick bases well. Grate ½ lb. cooking apples into a basin. Add 2 oz. sugar, grated rind and juice ½ lemon, and 2 oz. sultanas. Mix well together. Fill centre of each tartlet with this mixture.

Cut out 12 tops for tarts, dampen edges well then place to cover apple mixture. Seal well. Bake as Eccles Cakes.

CREAM SLICES

Make 1 quantity of pastry and roll out to ¼-in. in thickness. Cut into strips 5-ins. wide and 2-ins. long. Bake as for Eccles Cakes, cool and sandwich together in pairs with a thin layer of raspberry jam and whipped cream. Top with glacé icing flavoured as desired.

Fruit and cream-filled Vol au Vent

Light and luscious cream-filled choux pastry buns

CHOUX PASTRY

See the pastry rise to a rich golden lightness, and watch how fast the pile of buns disappears. You'll know the effort was worth-while

This is the perfect pastry for light, cream-filled cakes and desserts. This method is easy to master if you follow the simple basic recipe. Try serving with fruit cream fillings for parties, or with ice cream and a hot fruit sauce.

BASIC RECIPE

Your recipe: 4 oz. plain flour; $\frac{1}{2}$ level teasp. salt; $\frac{1}{2}$ pt. water; 2 oz. butter; 2 large eggs.

Sift the flour and salt together. Put water and butter in pan, bring to boil. Add sifted flour and beat well. Return to heat, stirring all the time until mixture forms a ball. Remove from heat and beat in eggs, one at a time. Beat very hard. *Secret of success:* Lots of hard beating when adding egg.

CREAM BUNS

Spoon the mixture on to greased baking tins using 2 teasps. Bake in upper part of mod. hot oven, Mark 5, 375 deg. for about 30 mins., or until the buns are well risen, golden and crisp. Remove from oven and make a hole in side to allow steam to escape.

When cold, fill with whipped cream, using a piping bag fitted with plain nozzle. Ice with coffee flavoured glace icing. They may also be served without icing, in which case just dust them with icing sugar.

ECLAIRS

Make as for cream buns, but pipe on to a greased tin using a piping bag fitted with $\frac{1}{2}$-in. plain nozzle. Bake. When cold, fill with cream and ice with chocolate glace icing.

ORANGE RING

Make the basic mixture and pipe into a circle on greased baking sheet. Bake as for Cream Buns, but for about 40 mins. Remove the ring and slice across in half. Fill with cream and orange segments. Ice top with orange flavoured glacé icing, and sprinkle the top with chocolate vermicelli.

CHURROS

Add an extra 2 oz. of butter to mixture in pan, together with 2 oz. castor sugar. Flavour mixture with 1 teasp. vanilla essence. Put mixture into a forcing bag fitted with $\frac{1}{4}$-in. fluted nozzle. Pipe mixture into hot oil in long strips. Fry until golden brown, then drain on crumpled kitchen paper. Dredge thoroughly with castor sugar.

PROFITEROLES

Make and bake in the same way as for Cream Buns and whipped cream.

Serve as a dessert with hot chocolate sauce.

MOCHA FINGERS

Make as for Eclairs but fill with lightly whipped cream flavoured with coffee essence. Ice with melted chocolate.

ALMOND BUNS

Make as for Cream Buns but sprinkle the tops with chopped almonds before baking.

When cold split and fill with a thick custard flavoured with almond essence or, if preferred, use whipped cream.

STRAWBERRY CHOUX FLAN

Bake an 8-in. round of flan pastry. Make up $\frac{1}{2}$ quantity of choux pastry and bake as for Cream Buns making them very small. Arrange the buns round the edge of the pastry, holding them in place with a little strawberry jam.

Fill the centre of flan with frozen or drained canned strawberries and coat with a jam glaze.

Decorate with piped cream or serve with whipped cream.

A satisfying treat hot from
the oven is
this tempting Lardy Cake

YEAST MIXES

Baking with yeast is an old-fashioned delight that's fast coming back into favour.
There's a fascination in seeing the
dough rise in the bowl as a heady scent of baking fills the kitchen

BASIC RECIPE

You require: 1 lb. plain flour; 2 level teasp. salt; $\frac{1}{2}$ oz. fresh yeast or 2 level teasp. dried yeast; $\frac{1}{2}$ pt. warm water, 1 tbsp. of cooking oil.

Sift flour and salt into bowl. Blend fresh yeast with warm water, or sprinkle dried yeast over warm water to which 1 level teasp. of sugar has been added. Leave in a warm place for about 10 mins. until mixture is frothy. Make well in the centre of flour, and add yeast liquid and oil. Form mixture into a dough and knead into a ball. Turn dough on to lightly floured board and knead well for about 10 mins. Put dough into covered bowl. Leave in a warm place for about $\frac{1}{4}$ hour until risen to twice its original size. Turn dough on to a floured board and knead well. Divide into 12. Shape into balls. Put on greased baking sheets. Cover. Put to rise as before. Bake 20-30 mins., Mark 7, 425 degs.

Secret of success: Use a strong plain flour and knead well to make dough elastic. Use only *warm* not hot liquid for mixing and put to rise in a *warm* not hot place—or yeast will be 'killed' before the dough has risen.

LARDY CAKE

You require: 1 quantity of dough, 4 oz. lard; 4 oz. castor sugar, 3 oz. sultanas if liked.

Put the once risen dough onto a floured board and knead well. Roll out into a strip $\frac{1}{4}$ in. in thickness and 3 times as long as it is wide. Dot the top two thirds with 1 third of the lard, and sprinkle with 1 third of the sugar. Add 1 third of the sultanas if used. Turn the bottom third of the dough up and the top third down. Press the edges well together and give the dough a quarter turn. Repeat the rolling, adding, folding and turning processes twice more until all the lard, sugar and sultanas have been used.

Shape the dough into an oblong and press into an oiled tin measuring 8 ins. by 10 ins. Brush the top with oil and leave in a warm place to rise, until double in size. With a sharp knife, cut a criss-cross pattern over the dough, and again brush with oil. Sprinkle with sugar. Bake in the centre of a mod. hot oven, Mark 7, 425 deg., for approximately 30 mins.

14

MIXES AND ALL-IN-ONE

Saving time is often an important factor to the busy housewife, but if you've ten or 15 minutes to spare, here are some speedy ways of making cakes that still retain a real, home-made flavour

CAKE MIXES

Use cake mixes to save time when you're rushed . . . and they're so handy to keep in your store cupboard for when unexpected guests arrive.

APRICOT GATEAU

Make up a sponge mix according to directions on the packet. When cool, sandwich the cakes together with apricot jam and brush sides with melted apricot jam, then roll in chopped, toasted almonds. Brush top with more melted jam and arrange well-drained apricots on top. Glaze the top with a quick setting jelly glaze and decorate with blanched almonds.

COCONUT MADELEINES

Three-quarters fill 12 greased dariole moulds with a packet sponge mix, made according to the directions on the packet. Bake in a moderate oven, Mark 4, 350 deg., for 15-20 mins. or until firm and golden. Remove from tins on to a cooling tray. Trip tops so that they will stand up.

Heat 3 tbsp. of seedless raspberry jam in a small saucepan. Brush the cakes with the hot jam and toss in 2 oz. of desiccated coconut. Decorate tops with halved glacé cherries and angelica leaves.

RAISIN RUM LAYER

Make a sponge mix according to directions on the packet and add the grated rind of 1 small orange. Bake according to directions. Beat 1 tbsp. of rum into $\frac{1}{2}$ quantity of orange flavoured butter cream (p. 7), stir in 1 oz. of seedless raisins. Sandwich cakes with this. Spread with orange icing.

ALL-IN-ONE MIXES

This is an astonishing quick-to-make method and gives excellent results as well as saving time and energy. In fact it is so simple to bake this way that even the children could help.

Secret of success: It is essential to use luxury margarines or a whipped-up quick creaming white vegetable fat.

BASIC RECIPE

You require: 4 oz. luxury margarine or white vegetable fat, 4 oz. castor sugar; 2 standard eggs; 4 oz. self-raising flour; 1 level teaspoon of baking powder; flavouring.

Put the margarine or vegetable fat, sugar and eggs into a large bowl. Add flour, pinch of salt and baking powder, sifted together. Beat well with a wooden spoon for 2 mins. Add flavouring. Bake in two 6-in. sandwich tins.

CHOCOLATE SANDWICH

Make as basic recipe, but add 1 level tbsp. of cocoa, mixed with 2 level tbsp. of warm water and 1 teasp. of vanilla essence. Divide the mixture between two 6-in. sandwich tins. Bake in a slow or mod. oven, Mark 3, 325 deg., for 25-30 mins. or until cakes are firm. Sandwich together with chocolate butter cream and sprinkle top with sifted icing sugar.

CHERRY ALMOND CAKE

Add 4 oz. glacé cherries, 2 oz. of chopped blanched almonds and 1 teasp. of almond essence to mix. Put mixture into a 6-in. round cake tin and bake in a slow to mod. oven, Mark 3, 325 deg., for 1-1$\frac{1}{2}$ hrs.

BANANA FROSTED CAKE

Make the basic recipe, but stir in 2 mashed bananas and 2 extra oz. of self-raising flour. Bake in a 6-in. round cake as for Cherry Almond Cake and cool. Cover cake with lemon flavoured American frosting (recipe, page 7).

Quick to make and delicious to eat—Apricot Gâteau

FOR SPECIAL OCCASIONS

Here's a delicious centre-piece for any party, a Frosted Grape Meringue Gateau

For special occasions everyone likes to have a trick or two up their sleeve. Here are two of my favourite ways of serving feather-light sandwich cakes in their party dresses.

GRAPE MERINGUE GATEAU

You require: 2 6-in. sandwich cakes, 2 egg whites, 4 oz. castor sugar, 1 lb. black grapes, 2 oz. granulated sugar ½ pt. whipped cream.

Make 2 6-in. sandwich cakes (see p. 4). Whisk the egg whites until stiff and standing in peaks. Add 2 oz. of the castor sugar and whisk again until the mixture will retain the impression of the whisk. Fold in remaining castor sugar.

Put the meringue into forcing bag fitted with ¼-in. open star nozzle. Pipe 5 finger meringues, 3 in. long on to a well-greased baking sheet. Pipe rest of mixture into small stars and dry the meringue in a very cool oven, Mark ¼, 240 deg. The meringues will stay white if cooked overnight with the oven door open.

Remove half the grapes from the main stem, in pairs, using scissors. Brush with a little egg white and toss in granulated sugar. Allow to dry.

Pip the remaining grapes and use to sandwich the sponge cakes together with a quarter of the cream. Spread the rest of the cream over the top and sides of the cake. Decorate sides of cake by marking in lines with a fork. Place the small meringues round the sides as in picture.

Place the finger meringues over the top and five bunches of frosted grapes in between.

Use the remaining bunches to decorate the base of serving dish. Keep in a cool place before serving.

CHOCOLATE MERINGUE LAYER

Make a Victoria Sandwich, (see p. 4) and stir in 2 oz. melted chocolate, after adding the eggs. Bake as for Victoria Sandwich. Make a meringue mixture (as left) but spread it into a Swiss roll tin to bake. Crush the cooked meringue. Sandwich the cake together with chocolate butter cream and half crushed meringue, and top with more butter cream and with the remaining crushed meringue.

Printed in England by Sun Printers Ltd., Watford and London.

Cod with creamed horseradish sauce

(Illustrated opposite)

Preparation time: 15-25 minutes

575 g / 1¼ lb fresh cod fillets
½ teaspoon salt
2 teaspoons lemon juice
600 ml / 1 pint water
100 ml / 4 fl oz cider
2 slices lemon
bunch mixed fresh herbs
1 apple
75 g / 3 oz grated horseradish or horseradish cream
pinch each salt and castor sugar
150 ml / ¼ pint double cream
lemon wedges and parsley to garnish

Rinse fish under cold water and dry on absorbent kitchen paper. Rub with the salt and sprinkle with lemon juice. In a saucepan, bring the water and cider to the boil with the lemon slices and herbs. Add the fish and simmer over low heat for 15 minutes. Remove the fish and keep warm. Peel, core and grate the apple and mix with horseradish, salt and sugar. Whip the cream until stiff and fold in the apple and horseradish mixture. Garnish the fish with lemon wedges and parsley and serve with the accompanying sauce.

Baked fish fillets

Preparation time: 15-25 minutes

675 g / 1½ lb fresh white fish fillets
1 tablespoon lemon juice
1 teaspoon salt
4 tablespoons water
300 g / 11 oz canned button mushrooms
2 tablespoons chopped parsley
25 g / 1 oz cheese, grated
15 g / ½ oz butter

Cod with creamed horseradish sauce (recipe above).

Set the oven at moderately hot (190 C, 375 F, Gas Mark 5). Place the fish on a plate, sprinkle with lemon juice and season with salt. Transfer to a shallow pan and steam or gently poach the fish, covered, in the measured water for about 10 minutes. Drain the mushrooms thoroughly. Arrange the cooked fish in an ovenproof dish, layer with mushrooms, and top with the parsley and cheese. Dot with the butter and bake in the oven for 8–10 minutes, or until the cheese has melted. Serve with rice or plain boiled potatoes and a crisp green salad.

Variation

The fish and mushrooms can be first heated through in the oven. Then add the butter and cheese, place under a medium-hot grill to brown.

Fish in white wine sauce

Preparation time: 15-25 minutes

150 ml / ¼ pint water
½ teaspoon salt
1 tablespoon lemon juice
575 g / 1¼ lb frozen white fish fillets
150 ml / ¼ pint white wine
bunch fresh dill or parsley
2 egg yolks
100 ml / 4 fl oz single cream
generous pinch of sugar

In a saucepan, bring the water to the boil with the salt and lemon juice. Lower the fish carefully into the water, cover and simmer for 12 minutes over gentle heat. Remove the fish, drain well and keep warm. Add the wine to the fish liquid and allow to come to a simmer. Wash, dry and chop the dill or parsley. Whisk the egg yolks with the cream and sugar. Beat 1 tablespoon of the fish liquid into the egg yolk mixture, then stir in the remaining fish liquid. Return to the saucepan and continue stirring until the sauce thickens but do not allow it to boil. Remove the saucepan from the heat, pour the sauce over the fish and sprinkle with dill or parsley before serving. Serve with Rice with mushrooms (see page 35) and a crisp green salad.

Tuna vols-au-vent

Preparation time: 15-25 minutes

4 individual vol-au-vent cases
½ onion
1 (184-g/6½-oz) can pimientos
1 (198-g/7-oz) can tuna
4 eggs, hard-boiled
pinch each salt, pepper, paprika pepper and
garlic salt
1 (198-g/7-oz) can shrimps
4 sprigs of parsley
lettuce leaves

Set the oven at moderately hot (190 C, 375 F, Gas Mark 5). Place the vol-au-vent cases on a baking sheet and heat gently in the oven. Meanwhile, peel and dice the onion, drain the pimientos and cut them into strips, reserving 4 to garnish. Drain the tuna well and flake with a fork in a bowl. Shell the eggs and chop them. Mix together the diced onion, pimiento strips, flaked tuna and chopped egg and season with salt, pepper, paprika and garlic salt.

Mix well and use to fill the vol-au-vent cases. Replace these in the oven to heat through. Meanwhile, drain and rinse the shrimps under cold running water. Pat dry on absorbent kitchen paper. Wash the parsley.

Garnish the warm pastry cases with the shrimps, the reserved pimiento strips and a sprig of parsley. Serve with Spinach soup (see page 13).

Lobster mayonnaise rolls

Preparation time: 15-25 minutes

1 pickled cucumber
bunch of parsley or dill
2 tomatoes
2 round crusty bread rolls
25 g/1 oz butter
2 tablespoons mayonnaise
2 tablespoons tomato ketchup
50 g/2 oz curd cheese
1 (225-g/8-oz) can lobster or crabmeat
½ lemon, sliced to garnish

Set the oven at hot (230 C, 450 F, Gas Mark 8) or heat the grill to maximum. Dice cucumber, wash and chop the parsley or dill. Wash and slice the tomatoes. Cut the bread rolls in half, hollow out and discard the soft middle and thinly spread the insides with butter. Place under the grill, cut side up, and lightly toast. Mix together the mayonnaise, ketchup, curd cheese and diced cucumber. Drain the lobster or crabmeat, rinse under cold running water, drain and flake with a fork. Blend into the mayonnaise mixture. Fill each warm, hollowed bread roll with lobster or crabmeat mayonnaise, garnish with parsley or dill and serve with a slice of lemon. Serve with Yogurt pea salad (see page 48).

Meat and poultry

Although grilling and frying meat are simple and quick methods of cooking, the time spent also depends on the quality of meat – good quality meat will cook evenly and faster than meat of a poorer standard. Remember, garnishes such as sprigs of parsley, dill or tomato slices are important as they turn a simple cooked dish into something special.

Sausage goulash

(Illustrated below)

Preparation time: 5-10 minutes

450 g/1 lb Frankfurter sausages
1 onion
1 (493-g/15.5-g) jar mixed pickles
2 tablespoons oil
1 (300-g/10-oz) can tomato soup
2 tablespoons tomato purée
salt and pepper
1 teaspoon dried marjoram

Slice the Frankfurters; peel and dice the onion. Drain the mixed pickles, then rinse briefly under cold running water and drain. Heat the oil in a saucepan or flameproof casserole and lightly fry the onion and mixed pickle. Add all the remaining ingredients and the Frankfurters to the onion mixture and stir well. Cover the pan and allow the goulash to simmer over a low heat for a further 5 minutes. Serve with plain boiled rice.

Sausage goulash.

Frankfurters 'in a blanket'

Preparation time: 5-10 minutes

8 Frankfurter sausages
4 slices processed cheese
8 streaky bacon rashers
1 tablespoon oil
tomato ketchup

Cut each Frankfurter half open, lengthways, to form a pocket, and cut each slice of cheese in half. Fold the cheese and fit each slice into a pocket. Wrap each Frankfurter in a bacon rasher and secure with a wooden cocktail stick. Heat the oil in a frying pan and fry the Frankfurters over high heat, turning constantly, until crisp and brown. Serve immediately with tomato ketchup and Sauté potatoes (see page 42).

Savoury ham slices

Preparation time: 5-10 minutes

25 g/1 oz butter
4 (100-g/4-oz) slices cooked ham
1 tablespoon canned crushed pineapple
1 tablespoon grated cheese
1 tablespoon desiccated coconut

Melt the butter in a frying pan over low heat, then gently fry the ham slices on either side for about 2 minutes. Sprinkle the pineapple, cheese and coconut over the ham in the pan. Replace the lid and continue to fry for a further 5 minutes without turning. Serve immediately with Pea soup with sausage (see page 8), French bread and a crisp green salad.

Pork chops with spiced apple sauce

Preparation time: 5-10 minutes

25 g/1 oz butter
4 (100–150-g/4–5-oz) cooked pork chops
100 ml/4 fl oz stock
250 ml/8 fl oz apple purée
4 tablespoons single cream
pinch each salt, pepper and ground ginger
dash Worcestershire sauce

Melt the butter in a frying pan and briskly fry the cooked pork chops on both sides. Remove, and keep hot, reserving the fat in the pan. Mix together the stock, apple purée, cream, dry seasonings and Worcestershire sauce and pour into the frying pan. Stir until thoroughly heated, then pour the sauce over the chops. Serve on a large warm dish with mashed potato and Cucumber salad (see page 44).

Quickie kebabs

Preparation time: 5-10 minutes

16 cocktail sausages
6 streaky bacon rashers
24 cocktail onions
4 maraschino cherries
2 tablespoons oil
2 level teaspoons paprika pepper

Set the oven at hot (230 C, 450 F, Gas Mark 8) or heat a grill to maximum. Cut each sausage in half. Flatten the bacon rashers by drawing them under the blade of a knife, then cut each in half and roll up. Thread on to the kebab skewers alternating with the sausage and onions, repeating the process until there is only room at the end for a cherry. Brush the kebabs with oil and sprinkle with paprika. Place on a baking sheet, put in the oven or under the grill and cook for about 8 minutes, turning the skewers so the kebabs cook evenly. Serve with Chicory salad (see page 45) and hot French bread.

Steak tartare with mixed pickles.

Steak tartare with mixed pickles

(Illustrated above)

Preparation time: 5-10 minutes

400–575 g/14 oz–1 lb lean minced steak
small capers
pickles, such as gherkins or dill pickle,
cucumber, cauliflower, pimientos, cabbage and
cocktail onions
1 tablespoon caraway seeds
1 tablespoon chopped parsley or chives
salt and pepper

Divide the steak into 4 portions and place on individual plates. Surround with small portions of capers and the pickles. Put a small mound of caraway seeds on each plate and sprinkle the meat with parsley or chives. Serve salt and pepper separately and garnish according to taste.

Frying meat

Meat, whether breadcrumbed or not and depending on personal taste and thickness, can be fried in 15 minutes or less. Sauces and side dishes are given in this chapter, but you can still prepare these dishes in 15–25 minutes.

A good steak should never be too thin, for a steak that is cooked right through in next to no time is regarded as sacrilege by steak-lovers. Meat intended for steaks should have been hung for some time. Always ask your butcher first what type of steak he recommends for frying or grilling.

Slices of meat weighing about 150 g/5 oz and about 1.5 cm/$\frac{3}{4}$ inch thick take about 4–7 minutes each side to cook and 2 minutes longer if breadcrumbed. Beef steaks weighing 200 g/7 oz take 2–6 minutes per side to cook depending on how well cooked they are required.

Here are some general hints

Slices of meat should be quickly rinsed under cold running water and dried with absorbent kitchen paper before cooking.

Meat slices which are not breadcrumbed should not be salted before frying.

Breadcrumbed meat slices should be salted first, breadcrumbed and then fried.

To speed cooking and to tenderise cutlets and escalopes, the meat may need beating out with a rolling pin before tossing in a little flour or beaten egg and breadcrumbs and frying. Beef steaks should not need beating.

Meat should first be fried over high heat to seal in the juices, but the heat should then be reduced to complete the cooking.

Use only pure fats, such as oil, lard or vegetable fat for frying. Butter tends to scorch easily at high temperatures.

Steak Quebec

(Illustrated opposite)

Preparation time: 10-15 minutes

4 (150-g/5-oz) fillet steaks
3 tablespoons oil
$\frac{1}{2}$ teaspoon salt
$\frac{1}{4}$ teaspoon paprika pepper
pinch garlic salt
1 (150-g/5-oz) can tomato purée
1 (224-g/8-oz) can peeled tomatoes, drained
1 large pickled cucumber
pinch dried basil
pinch each salt and castor sugar
4 lemon wedges
sprigs of parsley to garnish

Brush the steaks with the oil; heat any remaining oil in a frying pan and fry the steaks for 4 minutes on each side. Mix together the salt, paprika and garlic salt and sprinkle over both sides of the steaks. Put on a plate with meat juices and keep warm. Meanwhile mix the tomato purée with an equal quantity of water and heat through in a small saucepan. Chop the tomatoes and thinly slice the cucumber, and add to the tomato sauce. Season with the basil, salt and sugar. Pour the sauce over the steaks and serve each garnished with a wedge of lemon and a sprig of parsley. Serve immediately with plain boiled rice.

Entrecôte garni

Preparation time: 10-15 minutes

2 tablespoons oil
4 (200-g/7-oz) entrecôte steaks
salt and pepper
15 g/$\frac{1}{2}$ oz butter
4 eggs
1 tablespoon caviare or lumpfish roe (optional)
4 slices lean cooked ham, to garnish

Heat the oil in a frying pan. Gently press the steaks with your thumb to prevent too much shrinkage and fry for 4 minutes on both sides. Season well. In a separate frying pan, melt the butter and fry the eggs; season them to taste. Place the cooked steaks on warm plates, spread each steak with caviare or lumpfish roe, if used, and top with a fried egg. Garnish each entrecôte with a slice of ham and serve with French bread. Start with South sea salad (see page 46). Follow with Flambéed cherries (see page 74).

Russian steak

Preparation time: 10-15 minutes

2 tablespoons oil
4 (200-g/7-oz) rump or sirloin steaks
generous pinch each salt and pepper
15 g/$\frac{1}{2}$ oz butter
4 eggs
4 tablespoons single cream
1 teaspoon anchovy paste

Heat the oil until very hot in a frying pan and fry the steaks for 1 minute on each side, then reduce the heat and continue to fry for a further 3 minutes on each side. Season with salt and pepper and set aside on a plate to keep warm. Melt the butter with the remaining oil in the frying pan and fry the eggs. Arrange an egg on each steak and sprinkle lightly with salt. Mix the cream into the remaining fat, stir in the anchovy paste and pour the mixture around the steaks. Serve immediately with Simple tomato salad (see page 44).

Steak Quebec (recipe left).

Hunter's steak

(Illustrated opposite)

Preparation time: 10-15 minutes

---

2 tablespoons oil
4 (180-g/6½-oz) fillet steaks
½ teaspoon each salt and pepper
4 canned artichoke bottoms
4 eggs
1 (213-g/7½-oz) can button mushrooms,
drained and chopped
2 tablespoons chopped parsley

Heat the oil in a frying pan and fry the steaks for 5 minutes on each side. Season with half the salt and pepper, remove from the pan and keep warm. Drain the artichoke bottoms. Whisk the eggs with the remaining seasoning. Heat the mushrooms in the frying pan with the fat left over from the steaks, pour in the egg mixture, and stir until set. Place artichoke bottoms around the edge of the frying pan to heat through. To serve, set one artichoke bottom on each steak and top with some of the egg and mushroom mixture. Sprinkle over the parsley before serving with a green salad and French bread.

Steak au poivre

Preparation time: 10-15 minutes

---

4 tablespoons white peppercorns
4 (200-g/7-oz) fillet steaks
2 tablespoons oil
½ teaspoon each salt and celery salt
15 g/½ oz butter
75 ml/3 fl oz brandy

Coarsely crush the peppercorns, using the flat of the blade of a sharp knife or a pestle and mortar. Gently press the steaks into the peppercorns so they coat the meat well on both sides. Heat the oil in a frying pan and briskly fry the steaks on both sides. When cooked enough to suit, season well. Pour out the oil from the pan and add the butter. Pour the brandy into a ladle, warm it slightly and carefully set it alight, pouring the flaming brandy over the steaks. After one minute, turn the steaks over to extinguish any remaining flame. Serve with French bread or potato chips and Green salad with mayonnaise sauce (see page 46). Follow with Vanilla ice cream with hot chocolate sauce (see page 68).

Classic steak

Preparation time: 10-15 minutes

---

4 (200-g/7-oz) steaks (either fillet, rump or
sirloin)
2–3 tablespoons oil
salt and pepper

Rinse steaks quickly under cold running water and dry thoroughly with absorbent kitchen paper. Heat the oil in a frying pan and fry steaks on both sides. The exact time will vary according to taste. Season well. Serve with Corn salad (see page 44).

NOTE Frying times for steaks weighing 200 g/7 oz each:

For a rare steak, fry on each side for 1–2 minutes over high heat to seal the outside and barely cook the inside.

For a medium-done steak, fry on each side for 3–4 minutes over medium heat, leaving the inside slightly pink.

For a well-done steak, fry on each side for 4–5 minutes over medium heat so the meat is cooked right through and no pink can be seen inside.

Hunter's steak (recipe above).

Sherry kebabs

(Illustrated opposite)

Preparation time: 10-15 minutes

12 (3.5-cm/1½-inch) cubes fillet steak, about
450 g/1 lb in weight
15 g/½ oz dripping or lard
1 level teaspoon curry powder
½ teaspoon paprika pepper
generous pinch each salt and pepper
3 tablespoons soy sauce
1 tablespoon Kirsch
1 tablespoon sherry
1–2 tablespoons tomato ketchup

Thread 3 beef cubes on to 4 skewers and fry in the dripping or lard over a high heat for 1 minute, turning constantly. Season with the curry powder, paprika, salt and pepper and continue frying and turning for a few minutes. Pour a little hot water into the frying pan and stir to loosen any sediment. Stir in the soy sauce, Kirsch and sherry and continue to stir until the sauce is heated through. Add the ketchup and continue stirring until the sauce thickens. Pour the sauce into a sauce-boat and arrange the skewers on a plate. Serve the meat with green and tomato salads.

Maryland veal steak

Preparation time: 10-15 minutes

2 tablespoons oil
4 (150-g/5-oz) veal steaks
generous pinch each salt, pepper and
paprika pepper
175 g/6 oz canned sweet corn kernels, drained
4 tablespoons single cream

Heat the oil in a frying pan and fry the veal for 4 minutes on each side. Season with a little salt, pepper and paprika and set aside on to a plate to keep hot. In a small saucepan, over gentle heat,

Above: Sherry kebabs (recipe above); *Below:* Veal steaks in soy sauce (recipe above right); Apricot cream (page 66).

warm the sweet corn with the cream and any remaining fat from the frying pan. Season with salt and paprika and pour over the steaks to serve. Serve with Rice with mushrooms (see page 35).

Veal steaks in soy sauce

(Illustrated opposite)

Preparation time: 10-15 minutes

4 (100-g/4-oz) veal steaks
2 tablespoons oil
2 teaspoons soy sauce
salt and freshly ground pepper
1 (142-ml/5-fl oz) carton natural yogurt
1 tablespoon chopped parsley

Briefly rinse veal steaks under cold running water and dry with absorbent kitchen paper. Heat the oil in a frying pan and fry the steaks with the soy sauce for 5–6 minutes on each side. Sprinkle with salt and set aside on a serving dish to keep warm. Mix together with the fat remaining in the pan, the yogurt, pepper and parsley and heat through. Pour over the steaks to serve. Serve with bread or potato chips.

Escalopes of veal with tomatoes

Preparation time: 10-15 minutes

1 tablespoon oil
4 (75-g/3-oz) veal escalopes
½ teaspoon salt
freshly ground pepper
4 tomatoes

Heat the oil in a frying pan and fry the escalopes on one side only for 4 minutes. Mix the salt with a little pepper and sprinkle some over the veal. Turn the escalopes and cook on the other side for a further 4 minutes. Rinse and dry the tomatoes and cut each one in half. Sprinkle with a little more salt and pepper and fry for 4 minutes with the veal. Adjust the seasoning before serving.

Savoury cheese hamburgers.

Savoury cheese hamburgers

(Illustrated above)

Preparation time: 15-25 minutes

675 g/1 lb 8 oz minced beef
salt and pepper
1 egg, lightly beaten
50–75 g/2–3 oz Cheddar cheese, diced
1 tablespoon oil

Put the minced beef in a bowl, season well and bind with the beaten egg. Add the diced cheese and mix well. Divide the beef into 4 equal portions and shape each into a hamburger. Heat the oil in a frying pan and fry the hamburgers for about 4–5 minutes on each side, according to how well done you like your meat. Serve with cooked green vegetables and instant mashed potato.

Mexican meatballs

Preparation time: 15-25 minutes

450 g/1 lb minced beef
1 egg, lightly beaten
salt and pepper
2 tablespoons oil
25 g/1 oz butter
1 jar mini corn cobs (see note)
1 (184-g/6½-oz) can pimientos
2 tablespoons single cream
1 level teaspoon paprika pepper
pinch each salt and pepper
1 tablespoon tomato ketchup

In a bowl, combine the beef with the egg and seasoning to taste. Using a spoon, divide the beef into equal portions, rolling each into a ball about the size of an egg. Heat the oil in a large frying pan and cook the meatballs for about 8 minutes, turning frequently so they brown evenly. Set aside and keep hot. Melt the butter in a flameproof casserole and add the mini corn cobs, with a little of the liquid from the can, and heat through, stirring gently. Drain and chop the pimientos and add to the corn cobs in the casserole. Stir together the remaining ingredients, add them to the corn and allow to heat through. Serve the meatballs on a warmed dish or 4 individual plates and cover with the corn mixture. Serve with Continental potato salad (see page 42) or wholewheat bread. Follow with Advocaat fruit layer (see page 75).

NOTE If mini corn cobs are not readily available, substitute 1 (340-g/12-oz) can sweet corn kernels.

Fillet steak with parsley potatoes

Preparation time: 15-25 minutes

675 g/1½ lb small new potatoes, cooked in their skins
1 tablespoon dripping or oil
1 teaspoon salt
1 tablespoon chopped parsley
4 (150-g/5-oz) fillet steaks
1 tablespoon oil
½ teaspoon paprika pepper
4 tomatoes
15 g/½ oz butter
pepper

Carefully peel the cooked potatoes and cut any larger ones in half. Heat the dripping or oil in a frying pan, toss the potato in it and sprinkle with half the salt. Cover the pan and leave the potato to heat through over a low heat, stirring from time to time to prevent them from sticking. Add the parsley and toss to coat the potato. Keep warm. Rinse the meat under cold running water and dry with absorbent kitchen paper. Heat the oil in another frying pan and fry the fillets for 6 minutes on each side. Season with the remaining salt and the paprika, transfer to a dish and keep warm. Wash the tomatoes and, with a sharp knife, make a few incisions on the underside to prevent them splitting when cooked. Heat the butter in the juices remaining in the frying pan and add the tomatoes, season with pepper, cover and heat through over medium heat. Serve the fillets with tomatoes and parsley potatoes. Serve with Green salad with mayonnaise sauce (see page 46).

Madeira ragoût

Preparation time: 15-25 minutes

1 pickled cucumber
75 g/3 oz pickled beetroot
75 g/3 oz canned button mushrooms
1 tablespoon capers
250 g/9 oz fillet steak
200 g/7 oz lean pork
15 g/½ oz butter
1 tablespoon oil
½ teaspoon salt
¼ teaspoon pepper
½ teaspoon paprika pepper
4 tablespoons single cream
1 glass Madeira

Slice the cucumber and beetroot into thin strips. Drain and slice the mushrooms. Drain the capers. Remove any fat from the meat and cut into neat, even-sized pieces. Heat the butter and oil in a frying pan and gradually add the meat, shaking the pan and turning the meat until it is cooked and browned. Season with salt, pepper and paprika. Add the cucumber, beetroot, mushrooms and capers, mix well and cook over a low heat for about 10 minutes. Remove the pan from the heat, stir in the cream and Madeira. Serve immediately with bread and Chicory salad (see page 45).

NOTE If you have no Madeira, use sherry instead. A medium or dry sherry would be best.

Spicy pork cutlets

(Illustrated opposite)

Preparation time: 15-25 minutes

4 (100-g/4-oz) pork cutlets
½ teaspoon salt
¼ teaspoon pepper
1 tablespoon plain flour
1 egg, beaten
50 g/2 oz dry breadcrumbs
2 tablespoons oil
1 (213-g/7½-oz) can button mushrooms
4 tablespoons bought ready-made barbecue
sauce
2 tomatoes
50 g/2 oz Edam cheese, sliced
4 slices bread

Set the oven at hot (230 C, 450 F, Gas Mark 8), or heat a grill to maximum. Season the pork with salt and pepper, toss in the flour, then dip in beaten egg and finally in the breadcrumbs. Heat the oil in a frying pan and fry the cutlets for about 6 minutes on each side until crisp and brown. Drain and slice the mushrooms, put them into a saucepan with the barbecue sauce and gently heat through. Wash and halve the tomatoes. Set a tomato half on each cutlet and top with a slice of cheese. Lightly toast the bread on both sides and place a cutlet on each slice. Place on a baking tray and bake in the oven or under the grill until the cheese begins to melt. Pour the sauce over the cutlets and serve with Green salad with mayonnaise sauce (see page 46) and potato chips.

Savoury pork or chicken omelette

(Illustrated opposite)

Preparation time: 15-25 minutes

½ (450-g/1-lb) jar sauerkraut
200 g/7 oz smoked pork or chicken
1 tablespoon lard
1 small onion, chopped
4 eggs
1 teaspoon salt
2 tablespoons whisky
300 ml/½ pint water
50 g/2 oz plain flour
2 tablespoons dripping
300 ml/½ pint instant white sauce made-up
following the instructions on the packet
4 tablespoons tomato purée
25 g/1 oz grated cheese

Drain the sauerkraut and separate with a fork. Dice the pork or chicken. Melt the lard in a large frying pan and fry the onion until crisp. Add the sauerkraut and meat and stir well. Cover and simmer for 15 minutes.

In a bowl, whisk the eggs with the salt, whisky and water, then slowly stir in the flour to make a batter. In another frying pan, heat the dripping and make 4 pancake-like omelettes with the batter (see Spinach pancakes page 63). Transfer to a dish to keep them warm.

To the made-up white sauce, add the tomato purée and cheese and heat through. Arrange the omelettes on 4 individual plates, fill each with the sauerkraut mixture and fold over. Serve with the tomato and cheese sauce.

Opposite above: Spicy pork cutlets (recipe above left);
Below: Savoury chicken omelette (recipe above).

Veal cutlets Rosemarino.

Veal cutlets Rosemarino

(Illustrated above)

Preparation time: 15-25 minutes

150 ml/¼ pint water
4 large tomatoes
350 g/12 oz frozen peas
1 teaspoon salt
15 g/½ oz butter
4 (150-g/5-oz) best end veal cutlets
2 tablespoons oil
pepper
4 small sprigs fresh rosemary

Bring the water to the boil in a saucepan. Make a few incisions at the bottom of each tomato with a sharp knife. Pour over boiling water and leave for 2 minutes. Put the frozen peas into another saucepan with some of the salt and 2 tablespoons water, cover and cook over a low heat. Drain and

peel the tomatoes, cut off the top third and carefully hollow out the flesh. Melt the butter in a frying pan, add the tomatoes, cover and simmer gently for 5 minutes. Rinse the cutlets under cold running water and dry with absorbent kitchen paper. Heat the oil in a frying pan and fry the cutlets for 6 minutes on each side. Season with salt and pepper. Arrange the cutlets on a warm dish, garnish with rosemary (if fresh is not available, use ½ teaspoon dried). Drain the peas and use to fill the hollowed-out tomatoes. Serve the cutlets with the stuffed tomatoes arranged on one side and with Parsley potatoes (see page 29) as an accompaniment.

Variations

Coat the veal cutlets in beaten egg then dry breadcrumbs, or first in seasoned flour, then beaten egg and dry breadcrumbs mixed with grated Parmesan cheese. Fry the cutlets as above and serve with herb butter.

For a simple dish that is suitable for entertaining, serve the breadcrumbed veal cutlets with buttered peas tossed with strips of ham.

Chicken liver ragoût

Preparation time: 15-25 minutes

1 (425-g/15-oz) can peeled tomatoes
200 g/7 oz canned button mushrooms
50 g/2 oz butter
1 small onion, chopped
450 g/1 lb chicken livers
1 level teaspoon cornflour
½ teaspoon salt
¼ teaspoon pepper
100 ml/4 fl oz single cream
3 tablespoons chopped parsley

Thoroughly drain the tomatoes and mushrooms, reserving the liquid from both cans. Make the liquid up to 600 ml/1 pint with a little water. Melt the butter in a flameproof casserole and gently fry the onion. Add the chicken livers and fry gently on all sides for about 4 minutes. Mix the cornflour with a little of the reserved liquid and season well. Add the remaining liquid, the tomatoes, mushrooms and cornflour to the liver, stir to mix and bring to the boil, stirring constantly. Allow to boil gently for 1 minute before taking the ragoût off the heat. Stir in the cream and sprinkle with parsley to serve.

Spring chicken

Preparation time: 15-25 minutes

4 chicken breasts
2 teaspoons lemon juice
2 tablespoons oil
12 cocktail onions
200 g/7 oz canned button mushrooms, drained
1 (227-g/8-oz) can peeled tomatoes, drained
generous pinch each salt, pepper and dried
marjoram or oregano
4 tablespoons tomato ketchup

Place the chicken on a plate and sprinkle with the lemon juice. Heat the oil in a frying pan and fry the onions until just browned. Add the chicken breasts and fry over low heat for 6–7 minutes on each side. Arrange the mushrooms and tomatoes on top of the chicken, cover and allow to heat through. Season the ketchup and pour it over the chicken. Serve with mashed potato or buttered noodles and a crisp green salad.

NOTE Rashers of streaky bacon, derinded and fried until crisp can be added with the onions.

Chicken paprika

(Illustrated on page 34)

Preparation time: 15-25 minutes

1 onion
25 g/1 oz butter
15 g/½ oz plain flour
1 (397-g/14-oz) can peeled tomatoes
2 (184-g/6½-oz) can pimientos, drained
225 g/8 oz frozen peas
1 (1.5-kg/3-lb) cooked chicken
¼ teaspoon salt
generous pinch each salt and paprika pepper
150 ml/¼ pint soured cream

Peel and chop the onion. Melt the butter in a flameproof casserole and lightly fry the onion, stirring so that it does not stick. Dust with the flour while stirring lightly. Pour in the tomatoes with the juice from the can and mix well while it is heating through. Add the pimientos and frozen peas, cover the casserole and cook gently over a low heat. Cut the chicken into individual portions and heat up thoroughly in the sauce. Mix together the seasonings and soured cream and stir into the sauce just before serving. Serve with Fruit and nut salad (see page 48) and follow with Orange surprise (see page 66).

Rice, pasta and potatoes

Rice accompaniments

The following are useful ways to use up leftover ready-cooked rice.

Preparation time: 10-15 minutes

Rice with mushrooms

Thinly slice 75–100 g/3–4 oz mushrooms and fry gently in 25 g/1 oz butter. Add 575 g/1¼ lb cooked rice (made up from 190 g/6½ oz uncooked rice following the instructions on the packet). Cover and allow the rice to heat through. Stir in 1 tablespoon of chopped parsley before serving.

Curried rice

Reheat 575 g/1¼ lb cooked rice (see above recipe for uncooked quantity) in a covered colander over steam, if necessary. Melt 15 g/½ oz butter in a pan, add the rice and 1–2 teaspoons of curry powder to taste. Mix well and serve.

Risi Pisi

(An Italian rice dish.) Reheat 575 g/1¼ lb cooked rice (see Rice with mushrooms for uncooked quantity) in a covered colander over steam, if necessary. Melt 15 g/½ oz butter in a pan, add 100 g/4 oz frozen peas, cover and allow to heat through for about 6 minutes. Add the peas to the rice and mix well before serving.

Tomato rice

Reheat 575 g/1¼ lb cooked rice (see Rice with mushrooms for uncooked quantity) in a covered colander over steam, if necessary. Melt 15 g/½ oz butter in a saucepan, heat 3–4 tablespoons tomato purée in the butter and add the rice. Mix well and season before serving.

Hungarian savoury rice

Preparation time: 10-15 minutes

---

1 tablespoon oil
350 g/12 oz minced beef
1 small onion
100 ml/4 fl oz stock, made up with stock cubes if necessary
575 g/1¼ lb cooked rice (see note)
1 (425-g/15-oz) can peeled tomatoes
½ (340-g/12-oz) can asparagus tips
1 (213-g/7½-oz) can button mushrooms
pinch each salt, pepper and paprika pepper
2 tablespoons chopped parsley

Heat the oil in a flameproof casserole and lightly fry the meat until evenly browned. Peel and chop the onion and add it to the meat. Bring the stock to the boil in a saucepan, then stir it into the meat with the rice and tomatoes with their juice. Mix well. Drain the asparagus and the mushrooms and add them to the rice mixture. Season to taste, add the paprika and heat through. Serve hot, garnished with the chopped parsley. Finish with fruit yogurt.

NOTE 575 g/1¼ lb cooked rice is made up using 190 g/6½ oz uncooked rice following the instructions on the packet.

Opposite above: Ravioli with mixed vegetables (page 38); *Below:* Chicken paprika (page 33).

Rice salad

Preparation time: 10-15 minutes

2 small pickled cucumbers
1 banana
50 g/2 oz canned mandarin oranges
275 g/10 oz canned or frozen peeled prawns, thawed
450 g/1 lb cooked rice (see note)
1 (142-ml/5-fl oz) carton natural yogurt
2 tablespoons mayonnaise
few drops lemon juice
½ teaspoon salt
1 level teaspoon curry powder
generous pinch of castor sugar

Dice the cucumbers; peel and dice the banana. Drain and chop the mandarin oranges, reserving the juice. Drain the prawns and rinse under cold running water. Chop and mix together with cucumber, banana, mandarin oranges and cooked rice. Mix together yogurt, mayonnaise, 2 tablespoons of the reserved juice, lemon juice, salt, curry powder and sugar and fold into the rice mixture, making sure it is evenly distributed. Turn into a dish and serve with a crisp green salad.

NOTE For 450 g/1 lb cooked rice, use 150 g/5½ oz uncooked. Follow the instructions on the packet, then allow to cool before using for salad dishes.

Paprika rice

(Illustrated opposite)

Preparation time: 15-25 minutes

3 green peppers
2 tablespoons oil
400 g/14 oz minced beef
1 small onion
100 ml/4 fl oz stock, made with a stock cube if necessary
575 g/1¼ lb cooked rice (see note)
25 g/1 oz cheese, grated
½ teaspoon salt
½ teaspoon paprika pepper

Cut each pepper in half, deseed and remove and discard the core. Wash the flesh and cut into thin strips. Heat the oil in a large saucepan and fry the pepper for about 5 minutes, stirring all the time to prevent scorching. Add the meat and the peeled and chopped onion, and fry until the meat is evenly cooked and the onion transparent. Bring the stock to the boil in a small saucepan and add it to the meat mixture. Stir in the rice and cheese. Season with salt and paprika, mix well, cover and simmer over medium heat for about 5 minutes until the rice is heated through.

NOTE For 575 g/1¼ lb cooked rice, use 190 g/6½ oz uncooked. Follow the instructions on the packet, then allow to cool.

Curried rice with banana rolls

Preparation time: 15-25 minutes

225 g/8 oz rice
4 firm bananas
2 tablespoons dripping
1 teaspoon paprika pepper
4 (50-g/2-oz) slices lean cooked ham
4 tablespoons curry paste

Cook the rice following the instructions on the packet. Drain and briefly rinse in a colander or sieve. Meanwhile, peel the bananas and slice in half, lengthwise. Set the oven at hot (230 C, 450 F, Gas Mark 8). Melt the dripping in a frying pan, sprinkle the banana slices with paprika and gently fry them over low heat for about 1 minute. Put 2 banana halves together and wrap each pair in a slice of ham. Stir the curry paste into the remaining dripping in the pan and when it is well mixed, add the cooked rice, stirring to mix it in well. Place the curried rice in an ovenproof dish, arrange the ham and banana rolls on top and place in the oven or under a pre-heated hot grill to heat through for 5 minutes. Serve with Simple tomato salad (see page 44) or Green salad with mayonnaise sauce (see page 46).

Opposite above: Paprika rice (recipe left); *Centre:* Sweet and sour potato salad (page 42) served with fried fish fingers.

Cooking pasta

There are many different types of pasta available on the market, such as flat noodles, straight macaroni, elbow macaroni, spaghetti and shell and bow shapes that present many possibilities when making the various pasta dishes. Pasta is a useful storecupboard item for unexpected guests.

Whatever shape of pasta is used, it is important to follow the cooking instructions on the packet.

Here are some useful extra hints

Remember that for a main course, you should allow 75–100 g/3–4 oz pasta per person.

Cook all pasta in plenty of boiling salted water, rinse briefly under cold running water and drain well before serving. A teaspoon of oil in the cooking water will help prevent it sticking together while cooking.

Ravioli with mixed vegetables

(Illustrated on page 34)

Preparation time: 10-15 minutes

1 (440-g/15-oz) can ravioli in tomato sauce
400 g/14 oz canned mixed vegetables, drained
150 ml/¼ pint soured cream
100 g/4 oz cheese, grated
3 tablespoons chopped parsley
25 g/1 oz cold butter, flaked

Set the oven at hot (230 C, 450 F, Gas Mark 8). Fill an ovenproof dish with alternate layers of ravioli and vegetables, ending with ravioli. Pour the soured cream over the top and sprinkle with the cheese, then 2 tablespoons of the parsley. Dot with flaked butter and cook for 10 minutes or until the top is golden brown. Sprinkle with the rest of the chopped parsley and serve with Fruit and nut salad (see page 48) and follow with Orange surprise (see page 66).

Ravioli casserole

Preparation time: 10-15 minutes

1 (440-g/15-oz) can ravioli in tomato sauce
450 g/1 lb frozen peas
350 g/12 oz cooked ham
4 tablespoons dry breadcrumbs
6 tablespoons grated cheese
25 g/1 oz cold butter, flaked

Set the oven at hot (230 C, 450 F, Gas Mark 8). Open the ravioli, leave the lid lying loose on top and stand the can in a saucepan of boiling water to heat through. In another saucepan, place the peas with 2 tablespoons salted water and allow to cook for 3 minutes over low heat. Dice the ham. Lightly grease an ovenproof casserole. Add half the ravioli, the peas, then a layer of ham and finish with the remaining ravioli. Mix the breadcrumbs with the cheese and sprinkle over the ravioli. Dot the top with the flaked butter and bake in the oven for 8 minutes or until cooked through. Serve with Corn salad (see page 44) or Radish and apple salad (see page 46).

Mussel ragoût

Preparation time: 15-25 minutes

200 g/7 oz shell pasta
1 teaspoon salt
1 onion
400 g/14 oz canned mussels in brine
2 tablespoons oil
1 (397-g/14-oz) can peeled tomatoes, drained
generous pinch each salt, pepper and garlic salt

Cook the pasta with the salt following the instructions on the packet. Peel and dice the onion. Drain the mussels and reserve the liquid. In a frying pan, heat the oil and lightly fry the onion, tomatoes, mussels and a little of the reserved liquid. Cover and allow to warm through over low heat for 10 minutes. Meanwhile, drain the cooked pasta, and mix in the mussels and tomato mixture, seasoning to taste with salt, pepper and garlic salt. Serve immediately.

Chicken casserole with tomatoes.

Chicken casserole with tomatoes

(Illustrated above)

Preparation time: 15-25 minutes

---

200 g/7 oz spaghetti
1 teaspoon salt
1 (1.5-kg/3-lb) cooked chicken
1 onion
1 clove garlic
1 (184-g/6½-oz) can pimientos
1 (227-g/8-oz) can peeled tomatoes
2 tablespoons oil
150 ml/¼ pint red wine
2 tablespoons chopped parsley

Cook the spaghetti in boiling salted water following the instructions on the packet. Remove the meat from the chicken, discarding the bones and skin (save these for making stock), and chop the meat into small pieces. Peel and dice the onion. Peel, dice and crush the garlic. Drain the pimientos and tomatoes and chop in thin slices. Heat the oil in a flameproof casserole and lightly fry the onion and garlic, stirring continuously. Add the pimiento and tomato and continue to fry. Add the chicken and wine, cover the pan and heat through over low heat. Drain the spaghetti and rinse briefly under cold running water before adding to the chicken in the casserole. Toss and allow to heat through before garnishing with the parsley to serve.

If there is any chicken meat left over this can be cut up and added to a clear vegetable soup such as Vegetable noodle soup (see page 13).

Spaghetti bolognese

(Illustrated opposite)

Preparation time: 15-25 minutes

350 g / 12 oz spaghetti
1½ teaspoons salt
3 tablespoons olive oil
1 small onion, peeled and chopped
400 g / 14 oz minced beef
2 tablespoons tomato purée
1 (227-g / 8-oz) can peeled tomatoes, drained
¼ teaspoon pepper
1 teaspoon paprika pepper
100 ml / 4 fl oz white wine
100 g / 4 oz Parmesan cheese, grated

Cook the spaghetti with 1 teaspoon of the salt in boiling water, following the instructions on the packet. Heat the oil in a flameproof casserole and fry the onion. Add the meat and stir until evenly cooked and browned. Add the tomato purée and tomatoes and stir until thoroughly heated. Add the seasoning and wine, mix well, then cover and simmer for 10 minutes. Drain the spaghetti in a colander or sieve and rinse quickly under cold running water. Serve on a large dish with the sauce poured over and with the grated cheese handed separately. Accompany with a crisp green salad.

Ham noodles

Preparation time: 15-25 minutes

200 g / 7 oz noodles
15–25 g / ½–1 oz butter
1 onion, peeled and chopped
200 g / 7 oz cooked ham, cut in strips
100 ml / 4 fl oz soured cream
1 egg

Cook the noodles following the instructions on the packet and quickly rinse under cold running water. Drain well. Melt the butter in a frying pan

Spaghetti bolognese.

and fry the onion and ham. Add the noodles to the onion mixture and heat through. Whisk together the soured cream and egg, pour over the hot noodles and toss to allow the egg to set. Serve with a crisp green salad.

Potato accompaniments

Here are some simple but tasty ways to serve mashed potato. Use 1 (127-g / 4½ oz) packet instant mashed potato for each dish.

Preparation time: 5-10 minutes

Puréed potato with bacon

In a frying pan, lightly fry 50–100 g / 2–4 oz chopped streaky bacon and 1 peeled and chopped onion. Make up the mashed potato following the instructions on the packet and mix together with the bacon and onion. Season to taste.

Puréed potato with sauerkraut

Drain and chop 275 g / 10 oz sauerkraut and mix in 2–3 tablespoons unsweetened apple juice. Stir into the made-up mashed potato. Melt 15 g / ½ oz butter in a saucepan and add the potato. Heat through over gentle heat, stirring continuously.

Potato purée with horseradish

Peel, core and grate 1 large dessert apple and mix together with 2–3 tablespoons grated horseradish or horseradish cream (according to taste). Mix with the made-up mashed potato. Melt 15 g / ½ oz butter in a saucepan, add the potato and heat through over gentle heat, stirring continuously.

The following recipes make the most of leftover cooked whole potatoes. Estimate 175–225 g / 6–8 oz potatoes per person. The recipes will serve 4 as substantial accompaniments or buffet dishes.

Lyonnaise potatoes

In a frying pan, melt 25 g / 1 oz butter. Peel and dice 1 onion and lightly fry. Peel and slice the potatoes, sprinkle with salt and fry over a low heat on both sides until golden brown.

Sauté potatoes

In a frying pan, melt 40 g/1½ oz butter. Peel and slice the potatoes, season with salt and pepper and fry on both sides until golden brown.

Sauté potatoes with bacon

Prepare the potatoes as for Sauté potatoes, but fry with 100 g/4 oz chopped streaky bacon.

Variation

Add 1–2 lightly beaten eggs to the mixture, sprinkle with caraway seeds and stir until set.

Continental potato salad

Peel and slice the potatoes and pour over 175 ml/6 fl oz hot stock. Stir in 2 tablespoons chopped parsley, 1 tablespoon vinegar, 2 tablespoons oil and season with salt and pepper. Add sliced Frankfurters or sliced Mortadella or Continental ham sausage, or any chopped leftover meat. Mix together thoroughly and drain before serving warm or cold.

Herring and potato salad

Peel and slice the potatoes and season with salt and pepper. Add 225 g/8 oz diced cooked beetroot and 300 g/11 oz ready-made herring salad from a local delicatessen. Mix together well.

Sweet and sour potato salad

(Illustrated on page 37)

Peel and slice the potatoes and season with salt and pepper. Core and dice 1 apple, dice 1 pickled cucumber and 1 onion. Combine all these ingredients and add 1 tablespoon wine vinegar, 100 ml/4 fl oz mayonnaise, ½ teaspoon sugar and a generous pinch of dried marjoram, according to taste. Toss the salad with a few drops of lemon juice. This is particularly good served with fried fish fingers.

Savoury potato croquettes

(Illustrated opposite)

Preparation time: 10-15 minutes

1 (127-g/4½-oz) packet instant mashed potato
4 tablespoons grated Parmesan cheese
8 streaky bacon rashers
2 tablespoons dripping
1 Spanish onion
1 (227-g/8-oz) can peeled tomatoes, drained
2 tablespoons chopped parsley
1 tablespoon oil
1 tablespoon wine vinegar
175–225 g/6–8 oz cottage cheese
salt and pepper

Make up the instant mashed potato following the instructions on the packet. Mix in the Parmesan cheese and leave to stand for 5 minutes. In a frying pan, fry the bacon in its own fat until crisp and brown. Remove the bacon and heat the dripping in the same frying pan. Form the potato into 8 croquettes and fry in the dripping over low heat until crisp and brown on both sides. Peel and dice the onion; chop the tomatoes. Mix together the onion, tomato, parsley, oil, vinegar and cottage cheese, season to taste and serve with the croquettes in a separate bowl. Serve each potato croquette topped with a bacon rasher.

Savoury potato croquettes.

Salads

Corn salad

(Illustrated below)

Preparation time: 5-10 minutes

---

1 large carrot
2 apples
1 (198-g/7-oz) can sweet corn kernels
2 teaspoons lemon juice
½ teaspoon sugar
1 red pepper, deseeded and cut into strips
½ (142-ml/5-fl oz) carton natural yogurt
1 tablespoon oil
½ teaspoon salt
¼ teaspoon paprika pepper

Peel and wash the carrot, peel and core the apples and grate both. Drain the corn. Mix together the carrot, apple, corn, lemon juice, sugar and red pepper. Mix together the yogurt, oil, salt and paprika and fold the dressing into the salad. Serve in 1 large or 4 individual bowls with Classic steak (see page 25).

Cucumber salad

Preparation time: 5-10 minutes

---

1 small cucumber
1 (142-ml/5-fl oz) carton natural yogurt
salt and pepper

Wash, dry and finely slice the unpeeled cucumber into a bowl. Combine with yogurt and salt and pepper to taste and serve immediately.

Simple tomato salad

Preparation time: 5-10 minutes

---

4 large tomatoes
1 onion
¼ teaspoon each salt and pepper
1 tablespoon oil
1 teaspoon lemon juice

Wash and dry the tomatoes and slice thinly. Peel and dice the onion. Arrange the tomato slices on a plate and sprinkle with salt, pepper and diced onion. Mix together the oil and lemon juice and pour evenly over the salad before serving.

Corn salad.

Chicory salad

Preparation time: 5-10 minutes

2 heads chicory
2 bunches radishes
½ cucumber
1 tablespoon oil
1 tablespoon white wine vinegar
1 tablespoon apple juice
1 tablespoon orange juice
½ teaspoon salt
¼ teaspoon pepper
2 tablespoons chopped parsley

Cut off the hard base stems of the chicory, halve the heads and wash and drain well before slicing. Wash, top and tail, then slice the radishes; wash and slice the unpeeled cucumber. Mix together the oil, vinegar, apple and orange juice, salt and pepper and stir into the salad ingredients. Sprinkle over the chopped parsley and toss lightly before serving.

Haricot and tomato salad

Preparation time: 5-10 minutes

200-g/7-oz canned haricot beans
1 (227-g/8-oz) can peeled tomatoes
1 large dessert apple
100 g/4 oz celeriac, sliced
1 tablespoon wine vinegar
2 tablespoons oil
generous pinch each salt, garlic salt and pepper
few drops Worcestershire sauce (see note)
2 tablespoons chopped parsley

Drain the beans. Drain the tomatoes and chop them. Peel, core and dice the apple. Mix these ingredients with the sliced celeriac. Mix the vinegar, oil, salt, garlic salt, pepper and Worcestershire sauce and gently stir this dressing into the salad ingredients. Put the salad into a bowl, toss and sprinkle with parsley to serve.

NOTE It is possible to substitute 1 medium onion, chopped, for the Worcestershire sauce.

Haricot bean salad

Preparation time: 5-10 minutes

200-g/7-oz canned haricot beans
1 (184-g/6½-oz) can pimientos
100 g/4 oz celeriac, grated
90 g/3½ oz Cheddar cheese, diced
4 tablespoons mayonnaise
1 teaspoon wine vinegar
½ teaspoon mustard
dash Worcestershire sauce
¼ teaspoon salt

Drain the haricot beans. Drain and chop the pimientos and mix together with the beans, celeriac and cheese. Combine the mayonnaise with the vinegar, mustard, Worcestershire sauce and salt. Fold the dressing into the salad and toss well before serving. Serve with wholewheat bread.

Cucumber fruit salad

Preparation time: 5-10 minutes

200 g/7 oz pickled cucumbers, drained
2 dessert apples
2 bananas
2 teaspoons lemon juice
1 small lettuce
2 tomatoes
50 g/2 oz curd cheese
2 tablespoons mayonnaise
1 tablespoon finely-chopped hazelnuts

Dice the cucumbers. Peel, core and dice the apples; peel and dice the bananas. Mix the fruit and sprinkle with the lemon juice to prevent discoloration. Separate the lettuce, removing any coarse outer leaves or hard stalk and wash and dry the rest. Tear into small pieces and add to the fruit. Wash, dry and dice the tomatoes and add these also. Mix together the curd cheese and mayonnaise and stir into the salad ingredients. Serve sprinkled with the hazelnuts.

Radish and apple salad

Preparation time: 5-10 minutes

small bunch radishes
2 small dessert apples
2 teaspoons lemon juice
1 level teaspoon castor sugar
generous pinch each salt and pepper
1 tablespoon wine vinegar
1 tablespoon oil
½ teaspoon mustard
2 tablespoons chopped parsley

Wash, trim and thinly slice the radishes. Peel, core and grate the apples. Mix together with the lemon juice, sugar, seasoning, vinegar, oil and mustard. Toss, and sprinkle with parsley.

Green salad with mayonnaise sauce

Preparation time: 5-10 minutes

1 crisp lettuce
2 tablespoons mayonnaise
2 tablespoons single cream
2 tablespoons wine vinegar
¼ teaspoon each sugar and salt
½ teaspoon paprika pepper

Separate the lettuce, removing any coarse outer leaves or hard stalk and tear the rest into small pieces. Wash under cold running water and drain. Mix together the remaining ingredients and toss gently with the lettuce just before serving.

Variations

Substitute lemon, orange or pineapple juice for the mayonnaise and continue as above.

Alternatively, make a dressing with 75 g/3 oz crumbled Danish blue cheese mixed with 6 tablespoons single cream, 1 teaspoon lemon juice and a generous pinch of pepper.

South sea salad

(Illustrated opposite)

Preparation time: 10-15 minutes

1 grapefruit
1 (198-g/7-oz) can shrimps
4 canned pineapple rings
50 g/2 oz button mushrooms
½ medium cucumber
225 g/8 oz artichoke bottoms
100 ml/4 fl oz single cream
1 teaspoon grated horseradish
1 tablespoon tomato ketchup
generous pinch each salt and pepper

Peel and dice the grapefruit flesh removing any pips. Drain and rinse the shrimps under cold running water. Drain the pineapple and dice; slice the mushrooms. Peel the cucumber, cut it in half lengthwise, then remove the seeds and slice. Drain and rinse the artichoke bottoms and cut each in half. Mix together the cream, horseradish, ketchup and seasoning. Toss all the salad ingredients together and divide into 4 individual bowls. Pour some dressing over each to serve.

Smoked mackerel salad

Preparation time: 10-15 minutes

1 green pepper
1 dessert apple
225 g/8 oz celeriac, peeled
1 pickled cucumber
200 g/7 oz smoked mackerel
½ teaspoon curry powder
100 ml/4 fl oz tomato ketchup

Halve and deseed the pepper, wash and cut it into thin strips. Peel and core the apple and cut it into strips. Chop the celeriac into thin slices, dice the cucumber and chop the fish into neat pieces. Combine these salad ingredients. Stir the curry powder into the ketchup and gently mix into the salad. Serve with French bread.

South sea salad (recipe above).

Fruit and nut salad

(Illustrated opposite)

Preparation time: 10-15 minutes

1 lettuce
2 tomatoes
1 banana
2 teaspoons lemon juice
100 g/4 oz celeriac, grated (optional)
3 canned pineapple rings
2 tablespoons oil
2 tablespoons finely-chopped mixed nuts
½ teaspoon salt
1 tablespoon chopped parsley
walnut half, to garnish

Separate the lettuce, removing any coarse outer leaves or hard stem. Tear into small pieces, wash under cold water and drain well. Wash and dry the tomatoes and cut each into 8. Peel and slice the banana and sprinkle with lemon juice to prevent discoloration. Mix together the lettuce, tomato, banana and grated celeriac, if used. Drain the pineapple and reserve the juice. Cut through the pineapple rings, horizontally, reserving one slice for garnish. Cut the remaining slices into small pieces and mix with the other salad ingredients. Mix together the oil, 2 tablespoons of the reserved pineapple juice, the nuts, salt and parsley and combine with salad. Place the reserved pineapple slice in the centre of the salad and garnish with the walnut.

Fish salad

(Illustrated opposite)

Preparation time: 10-15 minutes

4 rollmop herrings
150 g/5 oz canned tuna
1 small lettuce
6 tomatoes
3 eggs, hard-boiled
100 ml/4 fl oz buttermilk or soured cream
dash white wine vinegar
½ teaspoon sugar
pinch each salt, pepper and dried chervil

Briefly soak the herrings for a few minutes in cold water, then drain and cut into chunks. Drain the tuna reserving the oil. Remove any coarse outer leaves and hard stalk from the lettuce and wash and dry the rest. Rinse and dry the tomatoes and cut each into 8. Remove the shell from the eggs and chop. Whisk together the remaining ingredients and the reserved tuna oil. Lightly toss all the salad ingredients in the dressing and serve with jacket potatoes or Continental potato salad (see page 42).

Yogurt pea salad

Preparation time: 15-25 minutes

250 ml/8 fl oz water
generous pinch salt
300 g/11 oz frozen peas
100 g/4 oz lean cooked ham
2 eggs, hard-boiled
leaves of lemon balm, if available
1 tablespoon lemon juice
1 teaspoon castor sugar
pinch white pepper
1 (142-ml/5-fl oz) carton natural yogurt
2 tablespoons chopped parsley

Bring the water to the boil with the salt in a saucepan, add the peas, cover and simmer over gentle heat until cooked. Meanwhile, cut the ham into strips. Remove the shell from the eggs and cut each one into 8. Wash and chop some lemon balm, if available. Drain the peas and mix together with egg and ham.

Mix together the lemon juice, sugar, pepper and yogurt and stir gently into the salad ingredients. Garnish with parsley and lemon balm, if available, and serve with toast.

Opposite above: Fruit and nut salad (recipe above left);
Below: Fish salad (recipe left).

Snacks

Fried egg snack

Preparation time: 5-10 minutes

1 tablespoon oil
8 streaky bacon rashers
8 eggs
salt and pepper
4 slices wholewheat bread

Heat the oil in a frying pan and fry the bacon until crisp. Break an egg on to each bacon rasher and fry until the egg is cooked. Season with salt and pepper. Arrange 2 eggs and 2 bacon rashers on each slice of bread for serving.

Spicy egg on toast

Preparation time: 5-10 minutes

4 lettuce leaves
4 slices wholewheat bread
1 tablespoon sandwich spread
4 eggs, hard-boiled
50 g/2 oz curd cheese
1–2 teaspoons grated horseradish or
horseradish cream
pinch each salt and pepper
dash Worcestershire sauce
tomato ketchup (optional)

Wash the lettuce leaves and pat dry. Lightly toast the bread slices on both sides and spread with the sandwich spread. Remove the shell from the eggs and slice as thinly as possible. Place one lettuce leaf on each slice of toast and top with egg slices. Mix together the curd cheese, horseradish and seasoning. Add a dash of Worcestershire sauce and spoon this mixture over the egg slices. Swirl a little ketchup on each, if used. Serve with Bean soup (see page 11).

Corned beef snack

(Illustrated on page 12)

Preparation time: 5-10 minutes

4 slices bread
2 tablespoons oil
4 slices corned beef
4 eggs
15 g/½ oz butter
pinch each salt and pepper
8 anchovy fillets
1 tablespoon capers

Lightly toast the bread on both sides. Heat the oil in a large frying pan and fry the corned beef slices on both sides. Place each slice of beef on one slice of toast and keep warm.

Meanwhile, fry the eggs in the butter and season with salt and pepper. Place a fried egg on each slice of corned beef and arrange anchovy fillets and capers on top. Serve with Curry cream soup (see page 13) and Simple tomato salad (see page 44).

Roast beef rolls

(Illustrated opposite)

Preparation time: 5-10 minutes

1 (432-g/15½-oz) jar pickled vegetables, such as
cauliflower, cocktail onions and gherkins
8 slices cold roast beef

Chop half of the mixed pickles, and keep the rest whole. Divide the chopped mixture among the slices of roast beef and roll up. Serve with the remaining pickles on a separate dish and with French or wholewheat bread.

Roast beef rolls.

Toast tartare

Preparation time: 5-10 minutes

4 slices wholewheat bread
25 g/1 oz butter
1 teaspoon anchovy paste
400 g/14 oz very lean minced steak
2 egg yolks
¼ teaspoon each salt, pepper and paprika pepper
general dash Worcestershire sauce
4 canned anchovy fillets
a few capers

Lightly toast the bread on both sides. Cream the butter with anchovy paste and spread on the toast. In a bowl, mix together the steak, egg yolks, seasoning and Worcestershire sauce and divide among the buttered slices of toast. Garnish each with a rolled anchovy and a few capers.

Smoked ham on toast

Preparation time: 5-10 minutes

4 slices wholewheat bread
15 g/½ oz butter
1 small packet Petit Suisse medium-fat soft cheese
1 tablespoon single cream
¼ teaspoon curry paste
1 teaspoon ginger syrup from a jar of preserved ginger
generous pinch each salt and cayenne pepper
200 g/7 oz smoked ham, cut into strips
4 small pickled cucumbers

Lightly toast the bread on both sides and spread with the butter. Stir together the cheese, cream, curry paste, ginger syrup, salt and cayenne and spread on the slices of toast. Arrange the strips of ham on top, then cut each pickled cucumber into a fan shape and use to garnish each open sandwich. Serve with Cream of tomato soup (see page 10) and Fruit and nut salad (see page 48).

Roast pork with pineapple

Preparation time: 5-10 minutes

8 large thin slices white bread
25 g/1 oz butter
4 thin slices cold roast pork
2 canned pineapple rings
1 tablespoon mayonnaise
1 teaspoon grated horseradish
½ teaspoon chilli powder, or to taste
1 teaspoon tomato ketchup

Spread the bread slices thinly with the butter and top 4 slices with a slice of pork. Slice the pineapple rings in half, horizontally, and top each pork slice. Mix together the mayonnaise, horseradish, chilli powder and ketchup and fill the centre of each pineapple ring with this mixture. Cover the sandwiches with the remaining bread slices. Serve with Spinach soup (see page 13).

Hawaiian toast

Preparation time: 5-10 minutes

4 large lettuce leaves
4 slices bread
15 g/½ oz butter
2 teaspoons grated horseradish
½ (225-g/8-oz) can crushed pineapple
2 tablespoons mayonnaise
1 teaspoon mango chutney
65 g/2½ oz curd cheese
2 level teaspoons paprika pepper
8 slices ham, cut to fit toast

Wash the lettuce leaves under cold running water and drain. Lightly toast the bread on both sides. Mix together the butter and horseradish and spread on the toast. Mix about 1 tablespoon of the crushed pineapple with the mayonnaise, chutney, curd cheese and paprika. On top of each piece of toast, place a lettuce leaf, a slice of ham and spread with the mayonnaise and cheese mixture; top with another ham slice and cover with the remaining crushed pineapple. Serve with Cream of tomato soup (see page 10).

Left : Parma ham and melon sandwich (recipe below); *Right :* Tuna and shrimp sandwiches (page 58).

Parma ham and melon sandwich

(Illustrated above)

Preparation time: 5-10 minutes

4 large lettuce leaves
15 g/½ oz butter
4 slices wholewheat bread
8 slices Parma ham
½ honeydew melon
1 (312-g/11-oz) can mandarin segments, drained

Rinse the lettuce under cold running water and drain well. Butter the bread slices and place a lettuce leaf on each one with 2 slices of the ham. Remove the seeds from the melon, peel and cut the flesh into 8 wedges. Place 2 wedges on top of each open sandwich and garnish with segments of mandarin.

Sally's banana toast

Preparation time: 5-10 minutes

4 slices bread
2 bananas
1 teaspoon lemon juice
200 g/7 oz Cervelat sausage, cut in cubes
(see note)
3 tablespoons mayonnaise
pinch each salt and paprika pepper
½ teaspoon mustard
1 teaspoon tomato ketchup
2 teaspoons chopped parsley

Lightly toast the slices of bread on both sides. Peel and chop the bananas and sprinkle with lemon juice to prevent discoloration. Combine the sausage with the bananas, mayonnaise, seasoning, mustard, ketchup and parsley. Spread over the slices of toast and serve with Spinach soup (see page 13) and Chicory salad (see page 45).

NOTE Cervelat sausage is a sausage made of mixed pork, beef and bacon.

Welsh rarebit

Preparation time: 5-10 minutes

15 g/½ oz butter
4 slices bread
250 g/9 oz cheese, grated
4 tablespoons light beer or ale
2 teaspoons mild mustard
1 teaspoon Worcestershire sauce

Set the oven at hot (230 C, 450 F, Gas Mark 8) or heat a grill to maximum. In a frying pan, melt the butter and fry the slices of bread on one side only. Mix together the cheese, beer, mustard and Worcestershire sauce and spread the mixture on the unfried side of each slice of bread. Place in the oven or under the grill and heat through for a few minutes or until the top is bubbling and golden brown. Serve immediately with Speedy goulash soup (see page 13).

Soft cheese and onion snack

Preparation time: 5-10 minutes

300–400 g/11–14 oz curd cheese
100–150 ml/4–5 fl oz milk or single cream
½ teaspoon salt
¼ teaspoon pepper
40 g/1½ oz chopped mixed herbs (see note)
1 small onion
wholewheat, rye or crispbread for serving

Combine the curd cheese, milk or cream, seasoning and herbs. Peel and dice the onion and gently stir into the cheese. Chill thoroughly and serve with wholewheat, rye or crispbread.

NOTE If fresh herbs are not available, use 1 tablespoon dried herbs and a little chopped fresh mustard and cress or parsley.

Variations

Curd cheese with cucumber Mix the same amount of curd cheese with the juice of 1 lemon, ½ an unpeeled, finely-chopped cucumber, a bunch of finely-chopped dill, parsley or chives and salt and celery salt to taste. Chill before serving.

Tomato and curd cheese Mix the same amount of curd cheese with 2 (227-g/8-oz) cans peeled tomatoes, drained and finely-chopped, 1 peeled and diced onion and salt and pepper to taste. Chill.

Paprika curd cheese Mix the same amount of curd cheese with 1 deseeded and diced red and green pepper, 1 peeled and finely-diced onion, and chopped chives, salt and paprika pepper to taste.

Ham curd cheese Mix the same amount of curd cheese with 100–150 ml/4–5 fl oz milk or single cream, 200 g/7 oz finely-chopped cooked ham, chopped parsley and salt to taste. Before serving, mix in 6 finely-chopped cocktail onions.

Sausage and cheese rolls

Preparation time: 5-10 minutes

8 Frankfurter sausages
4 crusty bread rolls
8 slices processed cheese
1 (184-g/6½-oz) can pimientos, drained and cut in strips
8 lettuce leaves
150 ml/¼ pint mayonnaise
parsley sprigs

Set the oven at hot (450 F, 230 C, Gas Mark 8) or heat a grill to maximum. Place the Frankfurters in a saucepan and pour over boiling water to cover. Simmer for 5 minutes. Halve the bread rolls. Drain the Frankfurters and cut each in half. Place 2 Frankfurter halves, side by side, on each halved roll and cover with a slice of cheese. Garnish with pimientos and bake in the oven or under the grill, until the cheese has lightly melted. Meanwhile, wash and dry the lettuce leaves and arrange on individual plates. Add a toasted roll and garnish each with a little mayonnaise and a sprig of parsley.

German toasted snack.

German toasted snack

(Illustrated above)

Preparation time: 5-10 minutes

---

1 level teaspoon cayenne pepper
2 tablespoons whisky
4 slices lean smoked ham, cut to fit toast
1 level teaspoon castor sugar
4 slices bread, lightly toasted
1 (450-g/1-lb) jar sauerkraut
4 slices blue cheese
4 maraschino cherries

Set the oven at hot (230 C, 450 F, Gas Mark 8) or heat a grill to maximum. Stir the cayenne into the whisky and marinate the ham slices in the liquor for a few minutes. Remove and dry on absorbent kitchen paper. Add the sugar to the rest of the marinade and divide among the slices of toast. Place the ham on top and cover each with sauerkraut and cheese. Bake just long enough to allow the cheese to melt. Garnish with a cherry.

Springtime toast

Preparation time: 5-10 minutes

---

4 large lettuce leaves
4 slices wholewheat, black rye or
pumpernickle bread
15 g/$\frac{1}{2}$ oz butter
1 teaspoon anchovy paste
2 large tomatoes
150 g/5 oz cottage cheese with chives

Wash the lettuce leaves and pat dry. Lightly toast both sides of the bread. Mix the butter with the anchovy paste and spread on the toast. Wash, dry and slice the tomatoes, removing the cores, and arrange them on top of the toast. Pile each open sandwich with cottage cheese. Serve with Pea soup with sausage (see page 8) and a crisp green salad.

Smoked fish toast

Preparation time: 10-15 minutes

4 slices bread
15 g/½ oz butter
2 dessert apples
1 teaspoon lemon juice
½ teaspoon salt
3 teaspoons grated horseradish or
horseradish cream
200 g/7 oz smoked trout, mackerel or buckling
50 g/2 oz Cheddar cheese, sliced
2 level teaspoons paprika pepper

Set the oven at hot (230 C, 450 F, Gas Mark 8) or heat a grill to maximum. Toast the bread and spread with the butter. Peel, core and grate the apples, mix with the lemon juice, salt and horseradish and spread the mixture on the buttered toast. Cut the smoked fish into small pieces and divide between the toast. Top with cheese slices. Bake in the oven or under the grill for up to 5 minutes, until the cheese is bubbling. Sprinkle with paprika before serving. Serve with Onion soup (see page 11) and follow with Ice cream with fruit sauce (see page 68).

Niçoise toast

(Illustrated opposite)

Preparation time: 10-15 minutes

4 large slices bread
1 clove garlic
15 g/½ oz butter
1 (198-g/7-oz) can tuna
100 g/4 oz cooked French beans
1 (184-g/6½-oz) can pimientos, drained
12 stuffed green olives, halved
8 cocktail onions
1 jar mini sweet corn cobs
(optional)
100 g/4 oz Cheddar cheese

Set the oven at hot (230 C, 450 F, Gas Mark 8) or heat a grill to maximum. Lightly toast the bread on both sides. Halve the garlic and use the cut side to rub over the toast, then spread with the butter. Drain the tuna. Divide the beans over the buttered toast and top with the pimientos, halved olives, onions and corn cobs, if used. Flake the tuna with a fork and top each of the open sandwiches. Slice the cheese and place on top. Bake the sandwiches in the oven or under the grill for 5 minutes or until the cheese melts. Serve with Speedy goulash soup (see page 13).

Pepper toast

(Illustrated opposite)

Preparation time: 10-15 minutes

4 slices bread
2 small green peppers (see note)
12 stuffed green olives
200 g/7 oz garlic sausage
100 g/4 oz Jarlsberg cheese, grated

Set the oven at hot (230 C, 450 F, Gas Mark 8) or heat a grill to maximum. Lightly toast the bread on both sides. Wash and deseed the peppers, remove the core and cut into rings. Rinse the olives under cold running water, drain well and cut widthways into thin slices. Slice the garlic sausage and arrange on the toast. Cover each slice with pepper rings and grated cheese. Top with sliced olives and place in the oven or under the grill until the cheese melts. Serve with Onion soup (see page 11) and follow with Sweet fruit omelette (see page 76) for dessert.

NOTE If cooked or blanched peppers are preferred, bring the rings to the boil in a saucepan of cold water and allow to boil for 1–2 minutes before draining well and arranging over the garlic sausage.

Opposite above: Niçoise toast; *Below:* Pepper toast.

Tuna and shrimp sandwiches

(Illustrated on page 53)

Preparation time: 10-15 minutes

4 large lettuce leaves
4 small sprigs dill or parsley
150 g/5 oz canned tuna
150 g/5 oz canned shrimp, drained
$\frac{1}{2}$ onion
1 green pepper
1 teaspoon anchovy paste
15 g/$\frac{1}{2}$ oz butter
4 slices wholewheat bread
250 g/9 oz canned artichoke hearts, drained

Rinse the lettuce and dill or parsley under cold running water and drain. Drain the tuna and rinse and drain the shrimp. Peel the onion and cut into rings. Halve the pepper, deseed and cut into rings. Beat the anchovy paste into the butter and spread on the bread slices. Place a lettuce leaf on each buttered slice, top with the tuna and artichoke hearts and then the pepper, onion rings and shrimp. Garnish each sandwich with a sprig of dill or parsley. Serve with Vegetable noodle soup (see page 13) and follow with Peach meringues (see page 74).

Mussel salad on toast

Preparation time: 10-15 minutes

2 eggs, hard-boiled
1 teaspoon lemon juice
2 teaspoons chilli sauce
2 teaspoons gin
1 tablespoon oil
generous pinch each salt, pepper, garlic salt
and sugar
100 g/4 oz canned peeled tomatoes
4 large slices bread
2 (100 g/4 oz) cans mussels in brine
2 tablespoons mayonnaise

Shell the eggs, chop the whites and mash the yolks with a fork. Mix the yolks with the lemon juice, chilli sauce, gin, oil, seasonings, sugar and chopped egg white. Drain and chop the tomatoes. Toast the bread on both sides. Drain the mussels and mix with the tomatoes and egg sauce. Spread a little mayonnaise on each slice of toast and top with the salad mixture.

Sausage on toast

(Illustrated opposite)

Preparation time: 10-15 minutes

4 slices bread
6–8 pork or beef sausages
15 g/$\frac{1}{2}$ oz butter
$\frac{1}{2}$ onion
2 tomatoes
4 slices processed cheese
a little paprika pepper

Set the oven at hot (230 C, 450 F, Gas Mark 8) or heat a grill to maximum. Lightly toast the bread on both sides. Remove the sausage meat from the skins and spread thickly over the toast. Heat the butter in a frying pan and fry the toast with the sausage meat underneath. Remove and keep warm. Peel and cut the onion into rings; slice the tomatoes. In the sausage fat remaining in the pan, quickly fry the onion and tomato and arrange on the toast. Place a slice of cheese on top and bake in the oven or under the grill until the cheese just melts. Garnish with a sprinkling of paprika to serve.

Sausage on toast.

58

Eggs in piquant sauce

(Illustrated opposite)

Preparation time: 10-15 minutes

8 eggs, hard-boiled
packet instant white sauce to
make 1 pint
1–2 teaspoons dry mustard
½ teaspoon castor sugar
1 tablespoon wine vinegar
1 teaspoon grated horseradish or
horseradish cream
2 tablespoons chopped parsley

Remove the shell from the eggs and cut each egg in half. Make up the sauce according to the instructions on the packet and stir over the heat while it thickens. Add mustard, to taste, and stir in the sugar, vinegar and horseradish. When the sauce is thoroughly heated, add the halved eggs and carefully heat through without breaking them. Garnish with parsley and serve with mashed potatoes.

Variations

Eggs in savoury tomato sauce Heat 25 g/1 oz butter in a saucepan and add 1 tablespoon flour. Stir with a wooden spoon over a low heat for a few minutes until golden brown. With the pan off the heat, add 1 (150-g/5-oz) can tomato purée and 250 ml/8 fl oz water slowly, stirring continuously. Return to the heat and stir until the sauce has thickened. Season with salt, pepper and paprika. Add 250 ml/8 fl oz tomato juice and 6 tablespoons tomato ketchup, before carefully adding the halved eggs. Heat through before serving. (Illustrated opposite.)

Eggs in curry sauce Melt 25 g/1 oz butter in a saucepan, and stir in 1½ tablespoons flour. Stir with a wooden spoon over a low heat for a few minutes until golden brown. Stir in 2–3 teaspoons curry powder and slowly add 350 ml/12 fl oz stock. Stir continuously over the heat until the sauce thickens. Season with salt and pepper and finally add 250 ml/8 fl oz single cream. Carefully add the halved eggs to heat through before serving. (Illustrated opposite.)

Tomato and bacon omelette

Preparation time: 10-15 minutes

1 (397-g/14-oz) can peeled tomatoes
100 g/4 oz streaky bacon
4 eggs, lightly beaten
25 g/1 oz plain flour
4 tablespoons milk
½ teaspoon salt
¼ teaspoon pepper
1 small onion, chopped and fried until crisp
2 tablespoons chopped parsley

Drain the tomatoes. Chop the bacon and in a covered frying pan, fry over a low heat, in its own fat until crisp. Stir together the eggs, flour, milk and salt to make a runny batter (you may need to add a little water). Pour the batter over the crispy bacon in the pan and allow it to set slightly over the heat for a minute or two. Cover with the drained tomatoes, sprinkle with pepper and the fried onion and garnish with parsley. Replace the lid and cook over low heat for 5 minutes. Serve immediately on a warmed dish accompanied with a crisp green salad.

Clockwise: Eggs in savoury tomato sauce; Eggs in curry sauce; Eggs in piquant sauce (recipes above).

Artichokes with eggs.

Artichokes with eggs

(Illustrated above)

Preparation time: 10-15 minutes

---

225 g/8 oz canned artichoke bottoms
2 tomatoes
2 tablespoons oil
$\frac{1}{2}$ teaspoon salt
$\frac{1}{4}$ teaspoon pepper
4 eggs
2 tablespoons single cream
2 tablespoons tomato purée
2 tablespoons chopped parsley

Drain the artichokes and reserve the liquid. Wash, dry and cut each tomato in half. Heat the oil in a frying pan and fry the artichokes and tomatoes on both sides over a low heat. Mix the salt and pepper and sprinkle half over the tomatoes. Carefully break the eggs into the pan to fry, sprinkling them with the remaining seasoning. Meanwhile, mix the cream with 1 tablespoon of the reserved artichoke liquid, the tomato purée and parsley and pour over the eggs just before serving. Serve with French bread or potato chips.

Continental egg and sausage salad

Preparation time: 15-25 minutes

2 tomatoes
2 eggs, hard-boiled
1 pickled cucumber
1 apple
100 g/4 oz Mortadella or Italian ham sausage
1 tablespoon lemon juice
½ teaspoon salt
generous pinch pepper
50 g/2 oz curd cheese
2 tablespoons single cream
½ teaspoon mild mustard
1 teaspoon grated horseradish or
horseradish cream
1 teaspoon sugar
4 large slices bread
2 tablespoons chopped parsley

Make a small incision at the base of each tomato, place in a bowl and pour over boiling water; leave for 1–2 minutes. Shell the eggs and chop. Dice the cucumber; peel, core and dice the apple. Remove the skin from the sausage and dice the meat. Drain the tomatoes, remove the skin, and cut the flesh into small pieces. Mix with the egg, cucumber, apple and sausage. Add the lemon juice and seasoning. Mix together the curd cheese, cream, mustard, horseradish and sugar and fold into the salad ingredients. Lightly toast the bread on both sides and top each slice with the salad, then garnish with parsley. Serve with Haricot bean salad (see page 45) or as a main course with Savoury potato croquettes (see page 42) and a crisp green salad.

NOTE If this dish is prepared a day in advance, keep it covered in a refrigerator and add a little milk before serving.

Spinach pancakes

Preparation time: 15-25 minutes

1 (227-g/8-oz) packet frozen chopped spinach
2 tablespoons double cream
salt and pepper
pinch ground nutmeg
4 eggs
150 ml/¼ pint milk
50 g/2 oz plain flour
2 tablespoons dripping or oil

Heat up the chopped spinach, following the instructions on the packet. Drain thoroughly. Stir in the cream, seasoning and nutmeg and keep warm. Meanwhile, make the pancake batter. Whisk together the eggs and milk and a pinch of salt. Stir in the flour, a little at a time, to prevent lumps. Heat a little of the dripping or oil in a frying pan for each pancake. Pour in a quarter of the batter, and tilt the pan so that the batter covers the base. Allow the batter to set before loosening the sides. Carefully turn the pancake over and cook on the other side until set. Tip the pancake on to a warmed plate and repeat with the remaining fat or oil and batter to make 4 pancakes.

Fill each pancake with the creamed spinach mixture and either roll up or fold over to serve.

Variation

Savoury pancakes may be made with a variety of fillings such as fried chicken livers, canned button mushrooms or fried bacon and served with a crisp green salad. A variety of sweet pancakes can also be made, for dessert. Serve with apple purée and a pinch of ground cinnamon, or spread thickly with jam or simply cover with a mixture of cinnamon and sugar. Fill with slices of baked fruit in season, such as apple, banana, pears or peaches or fill with stewed fruit.

Spanish fried eggs.

Spanish fried eggs

(Illustrated above)

Preparation time: 15-25 minutes

---

100 g/4 oz streaky bacon
1 onion
1 clove garlic
1 green pepper
4 tomatoes
2 tablespoons chopped parsley
few drops Tabasco sauce
pinch each dried oregano or marjoram and salt
2 (150-g/5-oz) cans prawns, drained
4 eggs

Chop the bacon. Peel and dice the onion; peel and crush the garlic with a little salt. Halve and deseed the pepper, rinse and cut into strips. Wash and dry the tomatoes and cut each into 8. In a frying pan, gently fry the bacon in its own fat, add the onion and garlic and fry together, stirring continuously. Add the pepper, tomato and parsley, cover and simmer for 10 minutes. Mix in the Tabasco, oregano or marjoram and salt and add the prawns. Break the eggs over the vegetable mixture and cook over high heat until the eggs are set. Serve with rye or wholewheat bread.

Cheesy prawn toast

(Illustrated below)

Preparation time: 15-25 minutes

2 (150-g/5-oz) cans prawns
25 g/1 oz butter
4 slices bread
1 (241-g/8½-oz) can asparagus tips
2 egg yolks
100 ml/4 fl oz single cream
40 g/1½ oz cheese, grated
½ teaspoon salt
generous pinch pepper
sprigs of parsley

Set the oven at hot (230 C, 450 F, Gas Mark 8) or heat a grill to maximum. Briefly rinse the prawns under cold running water and drain well. Pat dry on absorbent kitchen paper. Melt half the butter in a frying pan and fry the bread slices on one side only. Remove to an ovenproof dish. In the same frying pan, add the remaining butter and the prawns and heat through for 1 minute, stirring continuously. Drain the asparagus, reserving the liquid. Add the asparagus tips to the prawns and heat through. Mix together the egg yolks, cream, cheese and seasoning, adding a little of the reserved asparagus liquid. Divide the prawn mixture over each untoasted side of the bread and pour over the sauce. Bake in the oven or under the grill for 8–10 minutes, or until the cheese begins to bubble and brown. Garnish with parsley. Serve with a crisp green salad and Curd cheese with peaches (see page 72) for dessert.

Hungarian eggs 'en cocotte'

Preparation time: 15-25 minutes

50 g/2 oz butter
150 g/5 oz smoked ham
1 (100-g/4-oz) piece Edam or Cheddar cheese
4 eggs
salt and pepper
4 tablespoons double cream
4 level teaspoons paprika pepper

Grease 4 cocottes or ramekins with the butter. Dice the ham and the cheese and scatter in the bottom of the dishes. Break an egg into each and season to taste. Beat the cream until just stiff, mix in the paprika and spoon over the eggs. Cover each cocotte with cooking foil, stand in a bain marie or a roasting tin with hot water that just comes half way up the side of the dishes. Place in a moderate oven (160 C, 325 F, Gas Mark 3) for about 15 minutes, or until the eggs are cooked. Serve with toast.

Cheesy prawn toast.

Desserts

Apple snow

Preparation time: 5-10 minutes

3 egg whites
2 level tablespoons powdered glucose
350 g/12 fl oz apple purée
juice of ½ lemon
1 tablespoon preserved cranberries

Whisk the egg whites until stiff and fold in the glucose. Mix together the apple purée and lemon juice and fold into the 'snow'. Serve in 4 individual glass bowls topped with a few cranberries.

Cherry nut mousse

Preparation time: 5-10 minutes

3 eggs, separated
1 tablespoon icing sugar
100 g/4 oz finely-chopped nuts
20 maraschino cherries, rinsed and dried
generous dash cherry brandy or Kirsch

Whisk the egg whites until stiff. Beat the yolks with the icing sugar until frothy and add the nuts. Chop the cherries finely and fold into the yolk mixture with the egg whites. Spoon into 4 individual bowls and chill slightly before serving.

Brandied pears

Preparation time: 5-10 minutes

4 canned pear halves
4 tablespoons preserved cranberries or blackcurrants
1 tablespoon lemon juice
3 tablespoons pear brandy or Kirsch
2 tablespoons desiccated coconut

Arrange the pear halves, cut side down, on 4 plates. Mix together the cranberries or black-currants, lemon juice and brandy or Kirsch and pour over the pears. Garnish with coconut before serving.

Orange surprise

Preparation time: 5-10 minutes

2 oranges
1 tablespoon powdered glucose or castor sugar
4 tablespoons advocaat
1 teaspoon coffee essence

Peel the oranges, removing the pith and pips and dice the flesh. Divide among 4 plates and sprinkle each with glucose or sugar. Mix together the advocaat and coffee essence and pour over the oranges to serve.

Apricot cream

(Illustrated on page 26)

Preparation time: 5-10 minutes

500 g/1 lb 2 oz canned apricot halves
150 ml/¼ pint white wine
150 g/5 oz curd cheese, or cream cheese with a little milk
5 tablespoons double cream
25 g/1 oz desiccated coconut

In a liquidiser, blend together the apricots with their juice and the wine. Blend in the curd or cream cheese and cream. Fill 4 individual bowls and garnish with the coconut.

Variation

Peaches can be used instead of apricots and topped with a few raspberries.

Melon fruit salad.

Melon fruit salad

(Illustrated above)

Preparation time: 5-10 minutes

1 honeydew melon
2 oranges
200 g/7 oz black grapes
juice of 1 lemon
pinch of ground ginger
1 tablespoon sugar, or to taste

Cut the melon in half, lengthways, discard the seeds, scoop out the flesh and cut into cubes. Peel and dice the oranges removing the pips. Wash and drain the grapes, patting them dry with absorbent kitchen paper. Mix together the fruit, adding the lemon juice, ginger and sugar to taste. Pile the fruit back into the hollowed-out melon shells.

Special fruit cocktail

Preparation time: 5-10 minutes

$\frac{1}{2}$ teaspoon lemon juice
2 (225-g/8-oz) cans fruit cocktail, drained
4 sponge fingers
75 ml/3 fl oz cherry brandy, fruit brandy
(for example, apricot) or orange liqueur
1 tablespoon chopped almonds

Add the lemon juice to the fruit cocktail and spoon into 4 individual glasses or small bowls. Crumble the sponge fingers and sprinkle with the brandy or liqueur. Top each fruit cup with this mixture and sprinkle with chopped almonds.

Variation

Juice from canned or frozen raspberries can be substituted for the brandy.

Vanilla ice cream with hot chocolate sauce

Preparation time: 5-10 minutes

1 (500-ml/17.6-fl oz) carton vanilla ice cream
100 g/4 oz golden syrup
100 g/4 oz plain chocolate

Cut the ice cream into 4 portions and place in individual glasses or bowls. Leave in the refrigerator while making the sauce. Heat together the golden syrup and chocolate in a double boiler until melted and thoroughly blended. To serve, stir the hot chocolate sauce and pour it over the ice cream. Serve immediately.

NOTE A little brandy may be added to the hot chocolate sauce. Also for a ginger sauce, combine 2 tablespoons finely-chopped preserved ginger with about 2 tablespoons of the syrup from the jar. Add to the chocolate sauce.

Blackcurrant ice bowl

(Illustrated opposite)

Preparation time: 5-10 minutes

1 (1-litre/35.2-fl oz) carton blackcurrant sorbet
150 ml/¼ pint double cream
100 ml/4 fl oz advocaat
4 ice cream wafers

Cut the sorbet into 4 portions and place in individual glass bowls. Whip the cream until stiff. Pour a little of the advocaat over each ice cream portion and top with a swirl of the whipped cream. Garnish with an ice cream wafer or wafer biscuit and serve immediately.

Ice cream with fruit sauce

(Illustrated left)

Preparation time: 5-10 minutes

25 g/1 oz butter
275 g/10 oz frozen raspberries
50 ml/2 fl oz cherry brandy or Kirsch
1 (1-litre/35.2-fl oz) carton ice cream,
flavour according to taste

Melt the butter in a saucepan over low heat, add the raspberries and heat through. Stir in the brandy or Kirsch and heat through. Divide the ice cream between 4 individual glasses or turn out on to a serving dish, and pour hot fruit sauce over before serving.

Ice cream with fruit sauce.

Blackcurrant ice bowl (recipe above).

Muesli

Muesli originated in Switzerland and is regarded worldwide as a health food. It has become a very popular breakfast food but here are some variations that make ideal desserts. They are all prepared in 5–10 minutes.

Apple and orange muesli

(Illustrated opposite)

Preparation time: 5-10 minutes

2 apples
2 oranges
1 tablespoon lemon juice
2 tablespoons milk
100 g/4 oz curd or cream cheese
4 tablespoons honey
2 tablespoons finely-chopped hazelnuts
25 g/1 oz cornflakes

Peel, core and dice the apples. Peel the oranges and dice the flesh. Mix together the lemon juice, milk, curd or cream cheese and honey. Combine the apple and orange and spoon into 4 individual bowls. Top with the honey mixture and sprinkle with chopped nuts and cornflakes.

Yogurt muesli

(Illustrated opposite)

Preparation time: 5-10 minutes

4 canned peach halves, drained
1 tablespoon lemon juice
2 (142-ml/5-fl oz) cartons natural yogurt
1 egg yolk
2 tablespoons honey
1 dessert apple, grated

Dice the peach halves. Mix together the lemon juice, yogurt, egg yolk and honey. Gently fold into the diced peaches, top with grated apple and serve in 4 individual bowls as a dessert.

Fruit muesli

(Illustrated opposite)

Preparation time: 5-10 minutes

100 g/4 oz canned crushed pineapple, drained
100 g/4 oz mandarin segments, drained and chopped
250 ml/8 fl oz apple purée
2 (142-ml/15-fl oz) cartons natural yogurt
3 tablespoons honey
3 tablespoons finely-chopped nuts (optional)

Mix together the pineapple and chopped mandarin segments. Stir in the apple purée and spoon the mixture into 4 individual bowls. Mix together the yogurt and honey and top each of the 4 bowls with this mixture. Garnish with chopped nuts, if used. Serve as dessert after Bean soup (see page 11).

Banana muesli

(Illustrated opposite)

Preparation time: 5-10 minutes

1 tablespoon lemon juice
50 ml/2 fl oz orange juice
3 bananas
2 (142-ml/5-fl oz) cartons natural yogurt
1 tablespoon Demerara or castor sugar
4 tablespoons rolled oats

Mix together the lemon and orange juice. Peel the bananas and slice thinly. Divide between 4 individual bowls, and pour the juices over. Stir together the yogurt and sugar and top the fruit bowls. Sprinkle with rolled oats to serve. Serve as a dessert with Cream of tomato soup (see page 10) or Welsh rarebit (see page 54).

Clockwise from far right: Apple and orange muesli; Fruit muesli; Banana muesli; Yogurt muesli (recipes above).

Yogurt

Yogurt is a very useful and versatile ingredient because it is rich in protein but relatively low in calories. The following recipes can be prepared in 5–10 minutes.

Pineapple yogurt

Preparation time: 5-10 minutes

1 (225-g/8-oz) can crushed pineapple
1 tablespoon lemon juice
1 tablespoon honey
2 (142-ml/5-fl oz) cartons natural yogurt
4 sponge fingers

In an electric mixer, combine the pineapple with the juice from the can, the lemon juice, honey and yogurt. Crumble the sponge fingers into the bottom of 4 individual bowls before adding the yogurt.

Apple yogurt

Preparation time: 5-10 minutes

250 ml/8 fl oz apple purée
2 (142-ml/5-fl oz) cartons natural yogurt
2 tablespoons blackcurrant syrup or concentrated blackcurrant drink
2 egg whites
1 tablespoon icing sugar
few small dry almond macaroons (optional)

Using an electric mixer, combine the apple purée, yogurt and syrup. In a separate bowl, whisk the egg whites until stiff, and stir in the icing sugar. Fold the sweetened egg whites into the yogurt mixture and serve in 4 individual bowls. Garnish with macaroons, if used.

Variation

As an alternative to apple purée, use 2 peeled, cored and grated apples and continue as above.

Hazelnut yogurt

Preparation time: 5-10 minutes

2 (142-ml/5-fl oz) cartons natural yogurt
200 g/7 oz hazelnuts, chopped
2 egg yolks
2 tablespoons powdered glucose or castor sugar

Mix 1 carton yogurt with the remaining ingredients. When thoroughly combined, add the rest of the yogurt and mix well. Serve in 4 individual bowls.

Curd cheese

Curd cheese is a versatile medium-fat cheese that is readily available and becoming very popular. Cream cheese can be substituted in the following recipes; however, remember cream cheese has more calories. All these desserts are prepared in 5–10 minutes.

Curd cheese with peaches

Preparation time: 5-10 minutes

2 whole fresh, or 3 canned peach halves
1 teaspoon lemon juice
200 g/7 oz curd cheese
1 tablespoon honey
2 tablespoons single cream

If using fresh peaches, peel and chop into small chunks. If using canned peach halves, drain and chop. Sprinkle with lemon juice to prevent discoloration. Combine all the ingredients and serve in 4 individual bowls.

Variations

Instead of peaches, use apricots (fresh, canned or dried and soaked) or stoned and halved plums.

Banana curd cheese

Preparation time: 5-10 minutes

200 g/7 oz curd cheese
½-1 tablespoon powdered glucose, or to taste
1 tablespoon milk
1 teaspoon honey
2 egg whites
1 banana
1 teaspoon lemon juice

Mix together the curd cheese, glucose, milk and honey in a bowl. Whisk the egg whites until stiff and fold carefully into the cheese mixture. Peel and slice the banana and sprinkle with lemon juice to prevent discoloration. Fold into the curd mixture and serve in 4 individual glasses or bowls.

Variation

Add a little cooked rhubarb to the banana for extra flavour; or a few chopped toasted nuts for a contrast in texture. If using a very ripe banana, mash with a fork before sprinkling with lemon juice.

Wine and lemon cream (recipe right).

Orange curd cheese

Preparation time: 5-10 minutes

1 large orange
200 g/7 oz curd cheese
1 teaspoon lemon juice
1 tablespoon castor sugar
2 tablespoons single cream

Peel the orange, remove any pith and cut into segments. Combine with all the remaining ingredients and serve in 4 individual bowls.

Wine and lemon cream

(Illustrated below)

Preparation time: 5-10 minutes

150 ml/¼ pint white wine
150 ml/¼ pint water
1 (69-g/2.4-oz) packet vanilla instant dessert whip
1 (142-ml/5-fl oz) carton natural or lemon yogurt
rind of 1 lemon and juice of ½ lemon
few drops yellow food colouring (optional)
150 ml/¼ pint double cream, whipped
1 tablespoon chopped pistachio nuts
thin lemon slices to garnish

In a bowl, mix together the wine and water. Add the dessert whip and whisk vigorously for about 1 minute, until the mixture thickens. Stir in the yogurt, lemon rind and juice and the food colouring, if used. Pour into 4 individual glass bowls and chill slightly. Decorate with swirls of the whipped cream, a sprinkling of nuts and a few lemon slices.

Flambéed bananas

Preparation time: 10-15 minutes

4 bananas
15 g/½ oz butter
1 tablespoon vermouth
1 tablespoon castor sugar
100 ml/¼ pint white rum
4 sponge fingers
4 tablespoons banana liqueur or apricot brandy

Peel the bananas and slice evenly. Melt the butter in a frying pan over low heat, add the vermouth and sugar and stir until warmed through. Add the bananas and simmer for 5 minutes over low heat, turning them over occasionally. Pour the rum into a ladle and warm over a match or candle flame before pouring over the bananas and setting alight. After 1 minute, extinguish the flame by turning the bananas over. Crumble the sponge fingers and divide between 4 individual bowls. Pour the liqueur over the sponge fingers and fill with the banana mixture.

Flambéed cherries

Preparation time: 10-15 minutes

2 (213-g/7½-oz) cans stoned morello cherries
25 g/1 oz butter
2 tablespoons Campari
2 level tablespoons castor sugar
175 ml/6 fl oz rum
100 ml/4 fl oz single cream
100 g/4 oz sponge fingers

Drain the cherries, reserving the juice. Melt the butter in a saucepan and mix in the Campari and sugar. Add the cherries and heat through for 5 minutes, shaking the pan continuously. Pour the rum over the cherries, set it alight and allow it to burn for about 15 seconds. Put out the flame by pouring in the cream and 100 ml/4 fl oz of the reserved cherry juice. Keep the saucepan over the heat for another minute to completely warm through the sauce. Crumble the sponge fingers into 4 individual glass bowls and pour the hot cherries on top.

NOTE It might be helpful to warm the rum before pouring over the cherries and igniting.

Variation

Hot flambéed cherries are delicious served over vanilla ice cream. In this case, omit the cream and sponge fingers. Brandy or Kirsch can be used instead of rum.

Peach meringues

Preparation time: 10-15 minutes

8 canned peach halves
2 teaspoons lemon juice
2 tablespoons raspberry jam
3 egg whites
1 teaspoon finely-grated lemon peel
100 g/4 oz icing sugar

Set the oven at hot (230 C, 450 F, Gas Mark 8) or heat a grill to maximum. Drain the peach halves. Mix together the lemon juice and jam and half fill each peach with some of this mixture. Whisk the egg whites until stiff and fold in the lemon peel and icing sugar. Put a little of the meringue mixture on each peach half, place on an ovenproof dish and bake in the oven or under the grill until the meringue turns golden brown.

Variations

Instead of canned peach halves, substitute fresh peaches, pineapple slices, apricot halves, peeled orange or apple slices, pear halves or fresh ripe berried fruits.

Curd cheese with raspberry sauce

(Illustrated below)

Preparation time: 10-15 minutes

2 eggs, separated
25 g/1 oz castor or vanilla sugar
200 g/7 oz curd or sieved cottage cheese
4 tablespoons icing sugar
2 tablespoons lemon juice
4 tablespoons fresh or canned orange juice
4 tablespoons raspberry jam

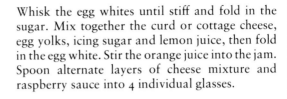

Whisk the egg whites until stiff and fold in the sugar. Mix together the curd or cottage cheese, egg yolks, icing sugar and lemon juice, then fold in the egg white. Stir the orange juice into the jam. Spoon alternate layers of cheese mixture and raspberry sauce into 4 individual glasses.

Advocaat fruit layer

Preparation time: 10-15 minutes

1 (500-ml/17.6-fl oz) carton vanilla ice cream
4 canned peach halves, drained
4 canned pineapple rings, drained
150 ml/$\frac{1}{4}$ pint double cream
100 g/4 oz canned or preserved morello cherries
150 ml/$\frac{1}{4}$ pint advocaat

Cut the ice cream into cubes and put into a bowl. Thinly slice the peach halves and 2 of the pineapple rings and mix together. Whip the cream until stiff. Fit a piping bag with a large star nozzle and fill with the cream. Drain the cherries. Put the ice cream into a liquidiser and blend until smooth. Stir in the advocaat. In a large bowl, make layers of advocaat cream and sliced fruit, finishing with a layer of advocaat cream. Pipe swirls of whipped cream and arrange the remaining pineapple rings on top. Arrange the cherries in the centre of the pineapple rings and serve immediately.

Curd cheese with raspberry sauce.

Sweet fruit omelette

Preparation time: 15-25 minutes

450 g/1 lb frozen strawberries or raspberries,
thawed
50 g/2 oz butter
a little sugar (optional)
6–8 eggs
pinch salt
icing sugar

Put the fruit in a frying pan with 15 g/½ oz of
the butter. Add the sugar, if used, cover and
warm through over low heat, stirring until the
fruit has softened. Meanwhile, in a bowl, whisk
together the eggs and salt. Melt the remaining
butter in another frying pan. Divide the beaten
egg into 4 to make 4 individual omelettes. Allow
the underside of each omelette to set before gently
loosening the edges. As each one is slipped out on
to a plate, fill one half with some of the warmed
strawberries and fold the other half over. Dust
with icing sugar and serve immediately.

Variation

Instead of strawberries or raspberries, use canned,
drained and sliced apricot halves, sliced peaches
or canned, drained blackberries or blackcurrants.

Mocha mousse

Preparation time: 15-25 minutes

4 eggs, separated
200 g/7 oz icing sugar
2 level teaspoons instant coffee powder
1 level tablespoon cocoa powder
15 g/1 oz powdered gelatine
2 tablespoons hot water

Whisk the egg whites until stiff. In a double boiler,
combine the icing sugar with the egg yolks, coffee
and cocoa and stir over a low heat until thick and
creamy. Remove from the heat. Dissolve the
gelatine in the hot water in a basin over a saucepan

of hot water. Blend into the egg yolk mixture and
fold in the egg white. Divide the mousse between
4 individual dishes and chill thoroughly before
serving.

Cherry meringue pudding

Preparation time: 15-25 minutes

300 ml/½ pint milk
½ vanilla pod
575 g/1 lb 4 oz cooked long-grain rice (see note)
100 g/4 oz castor sugar
500 g/1 lb 2 oz canned morello cherries,
drained and stoned
25 g/1 oz butter
4 egg whites
slivered almonds (optional)

Set the oven at hot (230 C, 450 F, Gas Mark 8) or
heat a grill to maximum. In a saucepan, gently
heat the milk with the vanilla pod. Once the milk
starts to simmer, remove the vanilla pod, add the
cooked rice and stir over a low heat until the milk
has been absorbed. Add 25 g/1 oz of the sugar and
most of the cherries, reserving a few for decora-
tion. Grease a 600 ml/1 pint pudding basin with a
little of the butter and fill with the rice mixture.
Chill thoroughly in the refrigerator for 2 hours to
set. Grease a shallow ovenproof dish with the
remaining butter and turn out the rice pudding.
Whisk the egg whites until stiff and fold in the
remaining sugar. Cover the rice mould with the
meringue and decorate with slivered almonds, if
used. Place in the oven or under the grill for 2–3
minutes until the meringue begins to brown.
Serve decorated with the reserved cherries.

NOTE For 575 g/1 lb 4 oz cooked rice, use 175 g/
6 oz uncooked rice.

Index

Parma ham and melon sandwich
53
Pea and ham soup 8
Savoury ham slices 20
Smoked ham on toast 52
Sweet and sour ham 30
Haricot bean salad 45
Haricot and tomato salad 45
Hawaiian toast 52
Hazelnut yogurt 72
Herring and potato salad 42
Horseradish, potato purée with
41
Horseradish sauce, cod with
creamed 17
Hungarian eggs 'en cocotte' 65
Hungarian savoury rice 35
Hunter's steak 25

Ice creams *see* Desserts

Kebabs:
Quickie kebabs 20
Sherry kebabs 27

Lobster mayonnaise rolls 18
Lobster soup 11
Lyonnaise potatoes 41

Madeira ragoût 29
Maryland veal steak 27
Mayonnaise sauce 46
Meat. *See also* Beef, Pork, Veal
To fry meat 21–2
Madeira ragoût 29
Melon:
Melon fruit salad 67
Parma ham and melon sandwich
53
Mexican meatballs 28
Mocha mousse 76
Mousse:
Cherry nut mousse 66
Mocha mousse 76
Muesli desserts 70
Mushroom:
Rice with mushrooms 35
Mussel:
Mussel ragoût 38
Mussel salad on toast 58

Niçoise toast 56
Noodle:
Ham noodles 41
Vegetable noodle soup 13

Omelettes:
Savoury pork or chicken omelette
30
Sweet fruit omelette 76
Tomato and bacon omelette 61
Onion:
Cream of onion soup 8
Onion soup 11
Soft cheese and onion snack 54
Orange:
Apple and orange muesli 70
Orange curd cheese 73
Orange surprise 66

Pancakes:
Spinach pancakes 63
Paprika curd cheese 54
Paprika rice 36
Parma ham and melon sandwich 53
Pasta. *See also* Noodles etc.
To cook pasta 38
Mussel ragoût 38
Pea:
Pea and ham soup 8
Pea soup with sausage 8
Risi pisi 35
Yogurt pea salad 48
Peach:
Curd cheese with peaches 72
Peach meringues 74
Pear:
Brandied pears 66
Pepper toast 56
Pineapple:
Hawaiian toast 52
Pineapple yogurt 72
Roast pork with pineapple 52
Pork:
Pork chops with spiced apple
sauce 20
Roast pork with pineapple 52
Savoury pork omelette 30
Spicy pork cutlets 30
Potato:
Continental potato salad 42
Fillet steak with parsley potatoes
29
Herring and potato salad 42
Lyonnaise potatoes 41
Potato purée with horseradish 41
Puréed potato with bacon 41
Puréed potato with sauerkraut 41
Sauté potatoes 42
Sauté potatoes with bacon 42
Savoury potato croquettes 42
Sweet and sour potato salad 42
Prawn. *See also* Scampi
Cheesy prawn toast 65
Puréed potato with bacon 41
Puréed potato with sauerkraut 41

Quickie kebabs 20

Radish and apple salad 46
Raspberry:
Curd cheese with raspberry sauce
75
Ice cream with fruit sauce 68
Ravioli casserole 38
Ravioli with mixed vegetables 38
Rice:
Curried rice 35
Curried rice with banana rolls 36
Hungarian savoury rice 35
Paprika rice 36
Rice with mushrooms 35
Rice salad 36
Risi pisi 35
Tomato rice 35
Roast beef rolls 50
Roast pork with pineapple 52
Russian steak 22

Salads:
Chicory salad 45
Continental egg and sausage
salad 63
Continental potato salad 42
Corn salad 44
Cucumber fruit salad 45
Cucumber salad 44
Fish salad 48
Fruit and nut salad 48
Green salad with mayonnaise
sauce 46
Haricot bean salad 45
Haricot and tomato salad 45
Herring and potato salad 42
Melon fruit salad 67
Mussel salad on toast 58
Radish and apple salad 46
Rice salad 36
Simple tomato salad 44
Smoked mackerel salad 46
South Sea salad 46
Sweet and sour potato salad 42
Yogurt pea salad 48
Sally's banana toast 53
Sauerkraut, puréed potato with 41
Sausage:
Continental egg and sausage
salad 63
Frankfurters 'in a blanket' 20
Pea soup with sausage 8
Quickie kebabs 20
Sausage and cheese rolls 54
Sausage goulash 19
Sausage on toast 58
Sauté potatoes 42
Sauté potatoes with bacon 42
Savoury cheese hamburgers 28